THE THREE FORMS
OF UNITY

THE THREE FORMS OF UNITY

*The Belgic Confession,
The Heidelberg Catechism &
The Canons of Dordt*

With an Introduction by Nick Needham

The Christian Heritage Series
Published by Canon Press
P.O. Box 8729, Moscow, Idaho 83843
800.488.2034 | www.canonpress.com

The Three Forms of Unity
Christian Heritage Series edition copyright ©2021
Translations of the Belgic Confession and Canons of Dort are taken from *The Constitution of the Reformed Dutch Church of North America* (1840). The translation of the Heidelberg Catechism is taken from the Tercentenary Edition published by the drection of the German Reformed Church in the United States of America (1859).
Introduction, copyright ©2021 by Nick Needham
The English translations were published in 1840 by G.W. Mentz & Son.

Cover design by James Engerbretson
Cover illustration by Forrest Dickison
Interior design by Valerie Anne Bost and James Engerbretson
Printed in the United States of America.

Library of Congress Cataloging-in-Publication Data

Needham, Nicholas R., writer of introduction. | Synod of Dort
   (1618-1619 : Dordrecht, Netherlands). Canones Synodi Dordrechtanae.
   English.
The three forms of unity : the Belgic Confession, the Heidelberg
   Catechism, & the Canons of Dordt / with an introduction by Nick Needham.
Belgic Confession. English.
Moscow, Idaho : Canon Press, [2021] | Series: Christian
   heritage series
LCCN 2021025818 | ISBN 9781954887176 (paperback)
LCSH: Reformed Church—Creeds. | Reformed
   Church—Catechisms—English.
Classification: LCC BX9428.A1 T47 2021 | DDC 238/.42—dc23
LC record available at https://lccn.loc.gov/2021025818

All rights reserved. No part of this publication may be reproduced, stored in a retrieval system, or transmitted in any form by any means, electronic, mechanical, photocopy, recording, or otherwise, without prior permission of the author, except as provided by USA copyright law.

21 22 23 24 25 26 27 28 29 30   10 9 8 7 6 5 4 3 2 1

CONTENTS

INTRODUCTION *by Nick Needham*

vii

THE BELGIC CONFESSION (1561)

1

THE HEIDELBERG CATECHISM (1563)

29

CANONS OF THE SYNOD OF DORT (1618-1619)

59

INTRODUCTION

The "Three Forms of Unity" is the name for three of the most significant and influential doctrinal standards to emerge from the Reformation and its aftermath: the Belgic Confession (1561), the Heidelberg Catechism (1563), and the Canons of Dort (1619). To the extent that these are unknown among Evangelicals today, it can only reveal a depth of ignorance that gravely impoverishes our knowledge of the richness of our theological heritage. The three documents together make up the collective confession of faith of the Dutch Reformed tradition—a tradition whose impact on the wider Reformed world has been almost incalculable.

THE BELGIC CONFESSION (1561)

The Belgic Confession was written by one of the forgotten heroes of the Reformation, Guido de Bres (1522-67). A native of Mons, whose personal study of the Scriptures persuaded him of the truth of the Reformation Gospel, De Bres spent several years in Protestant England from 1548 to 1552 as part of a congregation of Dutch Reformed refugees who had fled from Spanish persecution. (The Netherlands at that time—modern Belgium and Holland—were under Spanish sovereignty, and the intensely Roman Catholic Spaniards were very hostile to the Reformation.) However, starting in 1552 De Bres was back in the Netherlands, preaching, teaching, and church-planting, all of which he had to do under cover, owing to government opposition. Ultimately he would be martyred, executed in 1567 by the notorious Council of Blood. This body was set up by King Philip II of Spain to suppress Protestantism in the Netherlands, which it did (or attempted to do) with a brutality that has earned the Council enduring infamy in the annals of human carnage.

De Bres' literary monument was the Belgic Confession of 1561. In this manifesto, originally written in French, De Bres gave Dutch Protestants a confession of faith that demonstrated their catholic fidelity to the ecumenical creeds of the early Church, as well as their adherence to the Reformation understanding of the Gospel, as that found expression in its Reformed (Calvinist) rather than Lutheran articulation. De Bres was also careful to distinguish the Reformed faith from "Anabaptism," or the Radical Reformation, in today's parlance, whose roots and inspiration were largely alien to the Lutheran and Reformed faiths. Taking Calvin's 1559 Gallic Confession as a model, De Bres submitted his draft confession to several other theologians for approval, and then sent it to King Philip of Spain, in the forlorn hope of convincing Europe's most fiercely anti-Protestant monarch that his Dutch Protestant subjects were no threat to his Catholic rule. The Confession has 37 statements, chapters, or articles: the doctrine of the triune God (1-2, 8-11), Holy Scripture (3-7), Creation and Providence (12-13), Man (14), Original Sin (15), Eternal Election (16), the Person and Work of Jesus Christ (17-21), Salvation (22-26), the Church (27-36), and Eschatology (37).

When the Synod of Dort met in 1618-19 to settle the Arminian controversy (see below), it was suggested that the Synod might draft a new Reformed confession of faith to be a universal creed for the Reformed Churches across Europe. Instead the Synod adopted the Belgic Confession to serve this function. This gave the Belgic Confession a unique status among Reformed confessions of faith. Since that time, it has generally been recognized and honoured among the

Reformed Churches to a degree enjoyed by no other Reformed confession, as an articulation of Reformed belief peculiarly acceptable across the entire Reformed spectrum.

The text of the Belgic Confession was slightly revised by the French Reformed scholar-preacher Franciscus Junius (1545-1602) in 1565, and again at the Synod of Dort (see below) in 1619. It was translated into Latin for the international market in 1581. "Belgic" derives from the Latin "Gallia Belgica", the name for the province of the Roman Empire that embraced the southern part of the Netherlands. 16th century conflicts divided the Netherlands into the Roman Catholic Spanish Netherlands in the south—roughly modern Belgium—and the Protestant Dutch Republic in the north, which today has monopolized the name "Netherlands".

THE HEIDELBERG CATECHISM (1563)

The Heidelberg Catechism was the offspring of the surprising growth of the Reformed faith in Lutheran Germany. In 1559, the key south-western German territory known as the Rhenish Palatinate gained a new prince, Frederick III (1559-76). Frederick, one of the most sincere and godly Protestant rulers of the 16th century, made an intense study of the issues dividing Lutherans from Reformed, and was inclined to the Reformed side of the argument. To settle the matter, he held a five-day disputation in June 1560, which finally convinced Frederick that the Reformed were in the right. So began the new Reformed history of the Palatinate.

Frederick invited the illustrious Italian Reformer, Peter Martyr Vermigli (1499-1562), to become Heidelberg University's Reformed Professor of Theology, but Vermigli declined on grounds of old age, recommending instead one of his German students, Zacharias Ursinus (1534-83). Ursinus, a disciple of Lutheran Reformer Philip Melanchthon (1497-1560) as well as Vermigli, took up the position in 1561. Ursinus achieved a kind of literary immortality in the Reformed

Churches as the chief author of the Heidelberg Catechism, first published in 1563. A second and third German edition, each slightly revised, together with a translation into Latin, were published the same year. Marked by a moderate but lucid expression of Reformed theology and a warm evangelical spirit, the Catechism arguably combined all that was best in both the Lutheran and Reformed visions of Protestantism. This perhaps reflected Ursinus' debt both to Vermigli and Melanchthon. The Catechism went on to become the most widely accepted of all Reformed confessions, gaining recognition and use across the entire Reformed world, especially in Germany and the Dutch Republic.

The Catechism is divided into three parts: (i) *On Our Sin and Misery* (questions 1-11); (ii) *On Our Deliverance* (questions 12-85, containing an exposition of the Apostles' Creed); (iii) *On Our Thankfulness* (questions 86-129, containing an exposition of the Ten Commandments and the Lord's Prayer). The 129 questions of the Catechism were soon organized into fifty-two sections, so that one section per Sunday could be expounded to the churches on an annual basis.

THE CANONS OF DORT (1619)

The Synod of Dort (1618-19) was the most famous gathering of Reformed theologians in this history of the Reformed faith. Summoned by the Dutch government to settle a religious controversy that threatened to breed civil war in the Netherlands, the Synod was international in flavour, with representatives from the Netherlands, Germany, Switzerland, England, and Scotland (French representatives were also invited, but prevented from attending by their Roman Catholic monarch).

The controversy had been ignited by Dutch theologian Jacob Arminius (1560-1609) and his sympathizers ("Arminians"), who had tried to introduce "synergism" into the Dutch Reformed Church. Synergism—the view that the divine and human wills freely cooperate in salvation—ran counter to the "monergism" of the Reformation, which taught that the conversion of sinners originated in the sovereign "energy" of God, who alone is the source of new life in Christ. Although this was clearly taught by Calvin, the most celebrated exposition of monergism had actually come from Luther, in his 1525 classic *The Bondage of the Will*. Luther and Calvin alike had simply been following the great tradition of monergist theology flowing from Augustine of Hippo (354-430), greatest of the Western Fathers of the Church.

The Synod, meeting in Dort (or Dordrecht) in the south of Holland, went carefully through all the theological points raised by the Arminians, rejected them, and set out the Reformed response. The Canons of Dort, together with the Belgic Confession and Heidelberg Catechism, were then acknowledged as the doctrinal standard of the Dutch Reformed Church. They were also widely influential throughout the Reformed world. The French Reformed Church adopted the Canons as a binding confession. Elsewhere in Reformed Europe, although not adopted as binding, Dort's Canons were regarded as the "gold standard" of Reformed teaching on salvation. The English Puritan leader Richard Baxter (1615-91) famously praised the Synod of Dort (together with Britain's Westminster Assembly) in glowing terms: "the Christian world, since the days of the apostles, had never a synod of more excellent divines."

Since the Arminians had expressed their theology in five points in their Remonstrance of 1610, the Synod responded by working through these points, offering a Reformed view on each point. Here is the origin of the so-called "Five Points of Calvinism". We should be clear that these are not a summary of the whole of Reformed theology; they are simply Reformed theology's response to the five points of the Arminian Remonstrance on certain vital matters concerning human salvation. The Reformed faith is far wider and richer than the five points. Even so, the Canons of Dort were and remain the classical Reformed expression of the theology of the five points.

THE THEOLOGY OF THE THREE FORMS OF UNITY

Taken together, the Belgic Confession, Heidelberg Catechism, and Canons of Dort present a theology distinctively Reformed, putting clear blue water between the Reformed faith and its 16th century alternatives, whether Lutheran, Roman Catholic, or Radical/Anabaptist. Yet they do this in a way that combines moderation of spirit—at least toward Lutheranism—and a pastoral tone. The three documents were adopted by the Synod of Dort as a platform of unity among Reformed believers, especially in a Dutch Republic ravaged by the ecclesiastical and political conflicts of the Arminian controversy—here around these "forms of unity" people of the Reformed faith could gather, finding and confessing their family solidarity amid the confessional strife of the Reformation and post-Reformation era. Given the international status of Dort, this plea for unity on Reformed essentials spilled out beyond Dutch boundaries to the wider Reformed world.

It should be plain to any unprejudiced reader that the Three Forms of Unity are simply seeking to set forth the Holy Gospel of Jesus Christ in all its beauty, and the various implications of the Gospel for human thought and life. Anyone expecting to find a dry, abstract, narrow-spirited, over-complicated Calvinist "scholasticism" will be greatly disappointed. Readers will instead find a Calvinism that breathes the catholic spirit of the early church: one thinks of the strong affirmations of historic Trinitarian and Christological orthodoxy, and the endorsement of the evangelical witness of the early church Fathers, in the Belgic Confession. They will find a deep focus on the spiritual richness of the Apostles' Creed, the Ten Commandments, and the Lord's Prayer in the Heidelberg Catechism. In the Canons of Dort, they will discover a moderate expression of the doctrine of sovereign grace: the Canons insist that God sincerely calls to Himself all who hear His Gospel, and in the very midst of asserting the particularity of Christ's redeeming work (His purpose was to save His elect people) the Canons emphasize its universal sufficiency (should anyone perish, it is not due to any insufficiency or defect in the atonement, but due exclusively to the sinner's own unbelief).

This type of Calvinism—catholic, patristic, moderate, evangelical, pastoral—should go a long way toward dispelling the dark myths that so often surround the Reformed faith in the eyes of outsiders. It should also help free modern Calvinists from the distortions of their faith they have too frequently permitted to cloud their own vision: the narrow polemical obsession with the stricter side of the "five points," the Hyper-Calvinist denials of the freeness of the Gospel, the ignorance of (perhaps contempt for) the catholicity of the Reformed faith and its conscious indebtedness to the early church Fathers, the sometimes antinomian rejection of the Ten Commandments and Lord's Prayer as if structure were the enemy of spirituality. All of these warped misrepresentations are scattered to the winds by the Three Forms of Unity. May God grant that their republication in these pages will help to educate believers today in the depth, breadth, fullness, and fruitfulness of the Reformed faith as an expression of the Gospel.

~Dr. Nick Needham

THE BELGIC CONFESSION (1561)[1]

ARTICLE I. *That There is One Only God*
We all believe with the heart, and confess with the mouth, that there is one only simple and spiritual Being, which we call God; and that he is eternal, incomprehensible, invisible, immutable, infinite, almighty, perfectly wise, just, good, and the overflowing fountain of all good.

ARTICLE II. *By What Means God Is Made Known unto Us*
We know him by two means; first, by the creation, preservation and government of the universe; which is before our eyes as a most elegant book, wherein all creatures, great and small, are as so many characters leading us to contemplate "the invisible things of God," namely "His power and divinity," as the apostle Paul says (Rom. 1:20). All which things are sufficient to convince men, and leave them without excuse. Secondly, he makes himself more clearly fully known to us by his holy and divine Word, that is to say, as far as is necessary for us to know in this life, to his glory and our salvation.

---

1. Revised at the Synod of Dort in 1619

ARTICLE III. *Of the Written Word of God*
We confess that this Word of God was not sent, nor delivered by the will of man, but that "holy men of God spoke as they were moved by the Holy Ghost," as the apostle Peter says (2 Pet. 1:21). And that afterwards God, from a special care, which he has for us and our salvation, commanded his servants, the prophets and apostles, to commit his revealed word to writing; and he himself wrote with his own finger, the two tables of the law. Therefore we call such writings holy and divine Scriptures.

ARTICLE IV. *Canonical Books of the Holy Scripture*
We believe that the Holy Scriptures are contained in two books, namely, the Old and New Testament, which are canonical, against which nothing can be alleged. These are thus named in the Church of God. The books of the Old Testament are, the five books of Moses, viz.: Genesis, Exodus, Leviticus, Numbers, Deuteronomy; the books of Joshua, Ruth, Judges, the two books of Samuel, the two of the Kings, two books of the Chronicles, commonly called Paralipomenon, the first of Ezra, Nehemiah, Esther, Job, the Psalms of David, the three books of Solomon, namely, the Proverbs, Ecclesiastes, and the Song of Songs; the four great prophets Isaiah, Jeremiah, Ezekiel and Daniel; and the twelve lesser prophets, namely, Hosea, Joel, Amos, Obadiah, Jonah, Micah, Nahum, Habakkuk, Zephaniah, Haggai, Zechariah, and Malachi.

Those of the New Testament are the four evangelists, viz.: Matthew, Mark, Luke, and John; the Acts of the Apostles; the fourteen epistles of the apostle Paul, viz.: one to the Romans, two to the Corinthians, one to the Galatians, one to the Ephesians, one to the Philippians, one to the Colossians, two to the Thessalonians, two to Timothy, one to Titus, one to Philemon, and one to the Hebrews; the seven epistles of the other apostles, namely, one of James, two of Peter, three of John, one of Jude; and the Revelation of the apostle John.

ARTICLE V. *From Whence the Holy Scriptures Derive Their Dignity and Authority*
We receive all these books, and these only, as holy and canonical, for the regulation, foundation, and conformation of our faith; believing without any doubt, all things contained in them, not so much because the Church receives and approves them as such, but more especially because the Holy Ghost witnesses in our hearts, that they are from God, whereof they carry the evidence in themselves. For the very blind are able to perceive that the things foretold in them are fulfilling.

ARTICLE VI. *The Difference between the Canonical and Apocryphal Books*
We distinguish those sacred books from the apocryphal, viz.: the third book of Esdras, the books of Tobias, Judith, Wisdom, Jesus Syrach, Baruch, the appendix to the book of Esther, the Song of the three Children in the Furnace, the history of Susannah, of Bell and the Dragon, the prayer of Manasses, and the two books of the Maccabees. All of which the Church may read and take instruction from, so far as they agree with the canonical books; but they are far from having such power and efficacy, as that we may from their testimony confirm any point of faith, or of the Christian religion; much less detract from the authority of the other sacred books.

ARTICLE VII. *The Sufficiency of the Holy Scriptures, to Be the Only Rule of Faith*
We believe that those Holy Scriptures fully contain the will of God, and that whatsoever man ought to believe, unto salvation, is sufficiently taught therein. For, since the whole manner of worship, which God requires of us, is written in them at large, it is unlawful for any one, though an apostle, to teach otherwise than we are now taught in the Holy Scriptures: "nay, though it were an angel from heaven," as

the apostle Paul says (Gal. 1:8). For, since it is forbidden, to add unto or take away anything from the word of God (Deut. 4:2; Rev. 22:18-19), it does thereby evidently appear, that the doctrine thereof is most perfect and complete in all respects. Neither do we consider of equal value any writing of men, however holy these men may have been, with those divine Scriptures, nor ought we to consider custom, or the great multitude, or antiquity, or succession of times and persons, or councils, decrees or statutes, as of equal value with the truth of God, for the truth is above all; for all men are of themselves liars, and more vain than vanity itself. Therefore, we reject with all our hearts, whatsoever does not agree with this infallible rule, which the apostles have taught us, saying, "Try the spirits whether they are of God" (1 Jn. 4:1). Likewise, "if there come any unto you; and bring not this doctrine, receive him not into your house" (2 Jn. 1:10).

ARTICLE VIII. *That God Is One in Essence, yet Nevertheless Distinguished in Three Persons*
According to this truth and this Word of God, we believe in one only God, who is the one single essence, in which are three persons, really, truly, and eternally distinct, according to their incommunicable properties; namely, the Father, and the Son, and the Holy Ghost. The Father is the cause, origin and beginning of all things visible and invisible; the Son is the word, wisdom, and image of the Father; the Holy Ghost is the eternal power and might, proceeding from the Father and the Son. Nevertheless God is not by this distinction divided into three, since the Holy Scriptures teach us, that the Father, and the Son, and the Holy Ghost, have each his personality, distinguished by their properties; but in such wise that these three persons are but one only God. Hence then, it is evident, that the Father is not the Son, nor the Son the Father, and likewise the Holy Ghost is neither the Father nor the Son. Nevertheless these persons thus distinguished are not divided, nor intermixed: for the Father has not assumed the flesh,

nor has the Holy Ghost, but the Son only. The Father has never been without his Son, or without his Holy Ghost. For they are all three coeternal and co-essential. There is neither first nor last: for they are all three one, in truth, in power, in goodness, and in mercy.

ARTICLE IX. *The Proof of the Foregoing Article of the Trinity of Persons in One God*

All this we know, as well from the testimonies of holy writ, as from their operations, and chiefly by those we feel in ourselves. The testimonies of the Holy Scriptures, that teach us to believe this Holy Trinity are written in many places of the Old Testament, which are not so necessary to enumerate, as to choose them out with discretion and judgment. In Genesis, chap. 1:26, 27, God says: "Let us make man in our image, after our likeness," etc. "So God created man in his own image, male and female created he them." And Gen. 3:22: "Behold the man is become as one of us." From this saying, "Let us make man in our image," it appears that there are more persons than one in the Godhead; and when he says, "God created," he signifies the unity. It is true he does not say how many persons there are, but that, which appears to us somewhat obscure in the Old Testament, is very plain in the New.

For when our Lord was baptized in Jordan, the voice of the Father was heard, saying, "This is my beloved Son" (Matt. 3:17; Mk. 1:11): the Son was seen in the water, and the Holy Ghost appeared in the shape of a dove. This form is also instituted by Christ in the baptism of all believers. Baptize all nations, in the name of the Father, and of the Son, and of the Holy Ghost. In the Gospel of Luke, the angel Gabriel thus addressed Mary, the mother of our Lord, "the Holy Ghost shall come upon thee, and the power of the Highest shall overshadow thee, therefore also that holy thing, which shall be born of thee, shall be called the Son of God" (Lk. 1:35); likewise, "the grace of our Lord Jesus Christ, and the love of God, and the communion of the Holy

Ghost be with you" (2 Cor. 13:14). And there are three that bear record in heaven, the Father, the Word, and the Holy Ghost, and these three are one. In all which places we are fully taught, that there are three persons in one only divine essence. And although this doctrine far surpasses all human understanding, nevertheless, we now believe it by means of the Word of God, but expect hereafter to enjoy the perfect knowledge and benefit thereof in Heaven. Moreover, we must observe the particular offices and operations of these three persons towards us. The Father is called our Creator, by his power; the Son is our Saviour and Redeemer, by his blood; the Holy Ghost is our Sanctifier, by his dwelling in our hearts. This doctrine of the Holy Trinity, has always been defended and maintained by the true Church, since the time of the apostles, to this very day, against the Jews, Mohammedans, and some false Christians and heretics, as Marcion, Manes, Praxeas, Sabellius, Samosatenus, Arius, and such like, who have been justly condemned by the orthodox fathers. Therefore, in this point, we do willingly receive the three creeds, namely, that of the Apostles, of Nice, and of Athanasius: likewise that, which, conformable thereunto, is agreed upon by the ancient fathers.

ARTICLE X. *That Jesus Christ Is True and Eternal God*

We believe that Jesus Christ, according to his divine nature, is the only begotten Son of God, begotten from eternity, not made nor created (for then he should be a creature), but co-essential and coeternal with the Father, "the express image of his person, and the brightness of his glory" (Heb. 1:3), equal unto him in all things. He is the Son of God, not only from the time that he assumed our nature, but from all eternity, as these testimonies, when compared together, teach us. Moses says that God created the world; and John says that all things were made by that Word (John 1:3), which he calls God. And the apostle says that God made the worlds by his Son (Heb. 1:2); likewise, that

"God created all things by Jesus Christ" (Eph. 3:9). Therefore it must needs follow, that he who is called God, the Word, the Son, and Jesus Christ did exist at that time, when all things were created by him. Therefore the prophet Micah says, "His goings forth have been from of old, from everlasting" (5:2). And the apostle: "He has neither beginning of days, nor end of life" (Heb. 7:3). He therefore is that true, eternal, and almighty God, whom we invoke, worship and serve.

ARTICLE XI. *That the Holy Ghost Is True and Eternal God*

We believe and confess also, that the Holy Ghost, from eternity, proceeds from the Father and Son; and therefore neither is made, created, nor begotten, but only proceeds from both; who in order is the third person of the Holy Trinity; of one and the same essence, majesty and glory with the Father, and the Son: and therefore, is the true and eternal God, as the Holy Scriptures teach us.

ARTICLE XII. *Of the Creation*

We believe that the Father, by the Word, that is, by his Son, has created of nothing, the heaven, the earth, and all creatures, as it seemed good unto him, giving unto every creature its being, shape, form, and several offices to serve its Creator. That he does also still uphold and govern them by his eternal providence, and infinite power, for the service of mankind, to the end that man may serve his God. He also created the angels good, to be his messengers and to serve his elect; some of whom are fallen from that excellency, in which God created them, into everlasting perdition; and the others have, by the grace of God, remained steadfast and continued in their primitive state. The devils and evil spirits are so depraved, that they are enemies of God and every good thing, to the utmost of their power, as murderers, watching to ruin the Church and every member thereof, and by their wicked stratagems to destroy all; and are, therefore, by their own wickedness, adjudged to eternal damnation, daily expecting their horrible torments. Therefore we reject and abhor the error of the Sadducees, who deny the existence of spirits and angels: and also that of the Manichees, who assert that the devils have their origin of themselves, and that they are wicked of their own nature, without having been corrupted.

ARTICLE XIII. *Of Divine Providence*

We believe that the same God, after he had created all things, did not forsake them, or give them up to fortune or chance, but that he rules and governs them according to his holy will, so that nothing happens in this world without his appointment: nevertheless, God neither is the author of, nor can be charged with, the sins which are committed. For his power and goodness are so great and incomprehensible, that he orders and executes his work in the most excellent and just manner, even then, when devils and wicked men act unjustly. And, as to what he does surpassing human understanding, we will not curiously inquire into, farther than our capacity will admit of; but with the greatest humility and reverence adore the righteous judgments of God, which are hid from us, contenting ourselves that we are disciples of Christ, to learn only those things which he has revealed to us in his Word, without transgressing these limits. This doctrine affords us unspeakable consolation, since we are taught thereby that nothing can befall us by chance, but by the direction of our most gracious and heavenly Father; who watches over us with a paternal care, keeping all creatures so under his power, that not a hair of our head (for they are all numbered), nor a sparrow, can fall to the ground, without the will of our Father, in whom we do entirely trust; being persuaded, that he so restrains the devil and all our enemies, that without his will and permission, they cannot hurt us. And therefore we reject that damnable error of the Epicureans, who say that God regards nothing, but leaves all things to chance.

ARTICLE XIV. *Of the Creation and Fall of Man, and His Incapacity to Perform What Is Truly Good*

We believe that God created man out of the dust of the earth, and made and formed him after his own image and likeness, good, righteous, and holy, capable in all things to will, agreeably to the will of God. But being in honour, he understood it not, neither knew his excellency, but willfully subjected himself to sin, and consequently to death, and the curse, giving ear to the words of the devil. For the commandment of life, which he had received, he transgressed; and by sin separated himself from God, who was his true life, having corrupted his whole nature; whereby he made himself liable to corporal and spiritual death. And being thus become wicked, perverse, and corrupt in all his ways, he has lost all his excellent gifts, which he had received from God, and only retained a few remains thereof, which, however, are sufficient to leave man without excuse; for all the light which is in us is changed into darkness, as the Scriptures teach us, saying: "The light shineth in darkness, and the darkness comprehendeth it not" (Jn. 1:5), where St. John calls men darkness. Therefore we reject all that is taught repugnant to this, concerning the free will of man, since man is but a slave to sin, and has nothing of himself, unless it is given from heaven. For who may presume to boast, that he of himself can do any good, since Christ says, "No man can come to me, except the Father, which hath sent me, draw him" (Jn. 6:44)? Who will glory in his own will, who understands, that to be carnally minded is enmity against God? Who can speak of his knowledge, since "the natural man receiveth not the things of the spirit of God" (1 Cor. 2:14)? In short, who dare suggest any thought, since he knows that we are not sufficient of ourselves to think anything as of ourselves, but that our sufficiency is of God? And therefore what the apostle says ought justly to be held sure and firm, that "God worketh in us both to will and to do of his good pleasure" (Phil. 2:13). For there is no will nor understanding, conformable to the divine will and understanding, but that Christ has wrought in man; which he teaches us, when he says, "Without me ye can do nothing" (Jn. 15:5).

ARTICLE XV. *Of Original Sin*
We believe that, through the disobedience of Adam, original sin is extended to all mankind; which is a corruption of the whole nature, and a hereditary disease, wherewith infants themselves are infected even in their mother's womb, and which produces in man all sorts of sin, being in him as a root thereof; and therefore is so vile and abominable in the sight of God, that it is sufficient to condemn all mankind. Nor is it by any means abolished or done away by baptism; since sin always issues forth from this woeful source, as water from a fountain; notwithstanding it is not imputed to the children of God unto condemnation, but by his grace and mercy is forgiven them. Not that they should rest securely in sin, but that a sense of this corruption should make believers often to sigh, desiring to be delivered from this body of death. Wherefore we reject the error of the Pelagians, who assert that sin proceeds only from imitation.

ARTICLE XVI. *Of Eternal Election*
We believe that all the posterity of Adam being thus fallen into perdition and ruin, by the sin of our first parents, God then did manifest himself such as he is; that is to say, "merciful and just" (Ps. 116:5): "Merciful," since he delivers and preserves from this perdition all, whom he, in his eternal and unchangeable counsel of mere goodness, has elected in Christ Jesus our Lord, without any respect to their works: "Just," in leaving others in the fall and perdition wherein they have involved themselves.

ARTICLE XVII. *Of the Recovery of Fallen Man*
We believe that our most gracious God, in his admirable wisdom and goodness, seeing that man had thus thrown himself into temporal and eternal death, and made himself wholly miserable, was pleased to seek

and comfort him, when he trembling fled from his presence, promising him that he would give his Son, who should "be made of a woman," (Gal. 4:4) to bruise the head of the serpent, and would make him happy.

ARTICLE XVIII. *Of the Incarnation of Jesus Christ*

We confess, therefore, that God did fulfill the promise, which he made to the fathers, by the mouth of his holy prophets, when he sent into the world, at the time appointed by him, his own, only-begotten and eternal Son, who took upon him the form of a servant, and became like unto man, really assuming the true human nature, with all its infirmities, sin excepted, being conceived in the womb of the blessed Virgin Mary, by the power of the Holy Ghost, without the means of man, and did not only assume human nature as to the body, but also a true human soul, that he might be a real man. For since the soul was lost as well as the body, it was necessary that he should take both upon him, to save both. Therefore we confess (in opposition to the heresy of the Anabaptists, who deny that Christ assumed human flesh of his mother) that Christ is become a partaker of the flesh and blood of the children; that he is a fruit of the loins of David after the flesh; made of the seed of David according to the flesh; a fruit of the womb of the Virgin Mary, made of a woman, a branch of David; a shoot of the root of Jesse; sprung from the tribe of Judah; descended from the Jews according to the flesh; of the seed of Abraham, since he took on him the seed of Abraham, "and became like unto his brethren in all things, sin excepted," (Heb. 2:17, 4:15) so that in truth he is our Immanuel, that is to say, God with us.

ARTICLE XIX. *Of the Union and Distinction of the Two Natures in the Person of Christ*

We believe that by this conception, the person of the Son is inseparably united and connected with the human nature; so that there are not two Sons of God, nor two persons, but two natures united in one single person: yet, that each nature retains its own distinct properties. As then the divine nature has always remained untreated, without beginning of days or end of life, filling heaven and earth: so also has the human nature not lost its properties, but remained a creature, having beginning of days, being a finite nature, and retaining all the properties of a real body. And though he has by his resurrection given immortality to the same, nevertheless he has not changed the reality of his human nature; forasmuch as our salvation and resurrection also depend on the reality of his body. But these two natures are so closely united in one person, that they were not separated even by his death. Therefore that which he, when dying, commended into the hands of his Father, was a real human spirit, departing from his body. But in the meantime the divine nature always remained united with the human, even when he lay in the grave. And the Godhead did not cease to be in him, any more than it did when he was an infant, though it did not so clearly manifest itself for a while. Wherefore we confess, that he is very God, and very Man: very God by his power to conquer death; and very man that he might die for us according to the infirmity of his flesh.

ARTICLE XX. *That God Has Manifested His Justice And Mercy in Christ*

We believe that God, who is perfectly merciful and just, sent his Son to assume that nature, in which the disobedience was committed, to make satisfaction in the same, and to bear the punishment of sin by his most bitter passion and death. God therefore manifested his justice against his Son, when he laid our iniquities upon him; and poured forth his mercy and goodness on us, who were guilty and worthy of damnation, out of mere and perfect love, giving his Son unto death for us, and raising him for our justification, that through him we might obtain immortality and life eternal.

ARTICLE XXI. *Of the Satisfaction of Christ, Our Only High Priest, for Us*

We believe that Jesus Christ is ordained with an oath to be an everlasting High Priest, after the order of Melchisedec; and that he has presented himself in our behalf before the Father, to appease his wrath by his full satisfaction, by offering himself on the tree of the cross, and pouring out his precious blood to purge away our sins; as the prophets had foretold. For it is written: "He was wounded for our transgressions, he was bruised for our iniquities: the chastisement of our peace was upon him, and with his stripes we are healed. He was brought as a lamb to the slaughter, and numbered with the transgressors," (Is. 53:5, 7, 12) and condemned by Pontius Pilate as a malefactor, though he had first declared him innocent. Therefore: "he restored that which he took not away," and "suffered, the just for the unjust," (Ps. 69:4; 1 Pet. 3:18) as well in his body as in his soul, feeling the terrible punishment which our sins had merited; insomuch that "his sweat became like unto drops of blood falling on the ground" (Lk. 22:44). He called out, "My God, my God, why hast thou forsaken me?" (Matt. 27:46; Mk. 15:34) and has suffered all this for the remission of our sins. Wherefore we justly say with the apostle Paul that "we know nothing, but Jesus Christ, and him crucified" (1 Cor. 2:2); "we count all things but loss and dung for the excellency of the knowledge of Christ Jesus our Lord," (Phil. 3:8) in whose wounds we find all manner of consolation. Neither is it necessary to seek or invent any other means of being reconciled to God, than this only sacrifice, once offered, by which believers are made perfect forever. This is also the reason why he was called by the angel of God, Jesus, that is to say, Saviour, because he should save his people from their sins.

ARTICLE XXII. *Of Faith in Jesus Christ*

We believe that, to attain the true knowledge of this great mystery, the Holy Ghost kindles in our hearts an upright faith, which embraces

Jesus Christ, with all his merits, appropriates him, and seeks nothing more besides him. For it must needs follow, either that all things, which are requisite to our salvation, are not in Jesus Christ, or if all things are in him, that then those who possess Jesus Christ through faith, have complete salvation in him. Therefore, for any to assert, that Christ is not sufficient, but that something more is required besides him, would be too gross a blasphemy: for hence it would follow, that Christ was but half a Saviour. Therefore we justly say with Paul that we are justified by faith alone, or by faith without works (Gal. 2:16) However, to speak more clearly, we do not mean, that faith itself justifies us, for it is only an instrument with which we embrace Christ our Righteousness. But Jesus Christ, imputing to us all his merits, and so many holy works which he has done for us, and in our stead, is our Righteousness. And faith is an instrument that keeps us in communion with him in all his benefits, which, when become ours, are more than sufficient to acquit us of our sins.

ARTICLE XXIII. *Of Justification*

We believe that our salvation consists in the remission of our sins for Jesus Christ's sake, and that therein our righteousness before God is implied: as David and Paul teach us, declaring this to be the happiness of man, that God imputes righteousness to him without works. And the same apostle says that "we are justified freely by his grace, through the redemption which is in Jesus Christ" (Rom. 3:24). And therefore we always hold fast this foundation, ascribing all the glory to God, humbling ourselves before him, and acknowledging ourselves to be such as we really are, without presuming to trust in any thing in ourselves, or in any merit of ours, relying and resting upon the obedience of Christ crucified alone, which becomes ours, when we believe in him. This is sufficient to cover all our iniquities, and to give us confidence in approving to God; freeing the conscience of fear, terror and dread, without following the example of our first father,

Adam, who, trembling, attempted to cover himself with fig-leaves. And verily if we should appear before God, relying on ourselves, or on any other creature, though ever so little, we should, alas! be consumed. And therefore every one must pray with David: "O Lord, enter not into judgment with thy servant: for in thy sight shall no man living be justified" (Ps. 143:2).

ARTICLE XXIV. *Of Man's Sanctification and Good Works*

We believe that this true faith being wrought in man by the hearing of the Word of God, and the operation of the Holy Ghost, does regenerate and make him a new man, causing him to live a new life, and freeing him from the bondage of sin. Therefore it is so far from being true, that this justifying faith makes men remiss in a pious and holy life, that on the contrary without it they would never do anything out of love to God, but only out of self-love or fear of damnation. Therefore it is impossible that this holy faith can be unfruitful in man: for we do not speak of a vain faith, but of such a faith, which is called in Scripture, "a faith that worketh by love" (Gal. 5:6), which excites man to the practice of those works, which God has commended in his Word. Which works, as they proceed from the good root of faith, are good and acceptable in the sight of God, forasmuch as they are all sanctified by his grace: howbeit they are of no account towards our justification. For it is by faith in Christ that we are justified, even before we do good works; otherwise they could not be good works, any more than the fruit of a tree can be good, before the tree itself is good. Therefore we do good works, but not to merit by them, (for what can we merit?) nay, we are beholden to God for the good works we do, and not he to us, "since it is he that works in us both to will and to do of his good pleasure" (Phil. 2:13). Let us therefore attend to what is written: "when ye shall have done all those things which are commended you, say, we are unprofitable servants; we have done that which was our duty to do" (Lk. 17:10). In the meantime, we do not deny that God rewards our good works, but it is through his grace that he crowns his gifts. Moreover, though we do good works, we do not found our salvation upon them; for we can do no work but what is polluted by our flesh, and also punishable; and although we could perform such works, still the remembrance of one sin is sufficient to make God reject them. Thus then we would always be in doubt, tossed to and fro without any certainty, and our poor consciences continually vexed, if they relied not on the merits of the suffering and death of our Saviour.

ARTICLE XXV. *Of the Abolishing of the Ceremonial Law*

We believe, that the ceremonies and figures of the law ceased at the coming of Christ, and that all the shadows are accomplished; so that the use of them must be abolished amongst Christians; yet the truth and substance of them remain with us in Jesus Christ, in whom they have their completion. In the meantime, we still use the testimonies taken out of the law and the prophets, to confirm us in the doctrine of the gospel, and to regulate our life in all honesty, to the glory of God, according to his will.

ARTICLE XXVI. *Of Christ's Intercession*

We believe that we have no access unto God, but alone through the only Mediator and Advocate, Jesus Christ the righteous, who therefore became man, having united in one person the divine and human natures, that we men might have access to the divine majesty, which access would otherwise be barred against us. But this Mediator, whom the Father has appointed between him and us, ought in no wise to affright us by his majesty, or cause us to seek another according to our infancy. For there is no creature either in heaven or on earth who loveth us more than Jesus Christ; "who, though he was in the form of God, yet made himself of no reputation, and took upon him the form of a man, and of a servant for us, and was made like unto his brethren in all things" (Phil. 2:6). If then we should seek for another Mediator, who would be well affected towards us, whom could we find, who loved us more than he, who laid down his life for us, even when we were his enemies? And if we seek for one who has power and majesty, who is there that has so much of both as "he who sits at the right hand of his Father," (Col. 3:1) and who has all power in heaven and on earth? And who will sooner be heard than the own well beloved Son of God? Therefore it was only through distrust that this practice of dishonouring, instead of honouring the saints, was introduced, doing that, which they never have done, nor required, but have on the contrary steadfastly rejected according to their bounden duty, as appears by their writings. Neither must we plead here our unworthiness; for the meaning is not that we should offer our prayers to God on the ground of our own worthiness but only on the ground of the excellency and worthiness of the Lord Jesus Christ, whose righteousness is become ours by faith. Therefore the apostle, to remove this foolish fear, or rather mistrust from us, justly says, that "Jesus Christ was made like unto his brethren in all things, that he might be a merciful and faithful High Priest, to make reconciliation for the sins of the people. For in that he himself has suffered, being tempted, he is able to succour them that are tempted" (Heb. 2:17-18); and further to encourage us, he adds, "seeing then that we have a great High Priest, that is passed into the heavens, Jesus the Son of God, let us hold fast our profession. For we have not a high priest which cannot be touched with the feeling of our infirmities; but was in all points tempted like as we are, yet without sin. Let us therefore come boldly unto the throne of grace, that we may obtain mercy, and find grace to help in time of need" (Heb. 4:14-16).

The same apostle says, "having boldness to enter into the holiest, by the blood of Jesus; let us draw near with a true heart in full assurance of faith," (Heb. 10:19, 22) etc. Likewise, "Christ has an unchangeable priesthood, wherefore he is able also to save them to the uttermost, that come unto God by him, seeing he ever liveth to make intercession for them" (Heb. 7:24-25). What more can be required? since Christ himself says, "I am the way and the truth, and the life: no man cometh unto the Father but by me" (Jn. 14:6). To what purpose should we then seek another advocate, since it has pleased God, to give us his own Son as an advocate? Let us not for sake him to take another, or rather to seek after another, without ever being able to find him; for God well knew, when he gave him to us, that we were sinners. Therefore according to the command of Christ, we call upon the heavenly Father through Jesus Christ our own Mediator, as we are taught in the Lord's prayer; being assured that whatever we ask of the Father in his name, will be granted us.

ARTICLE XXVII. *Of the Catholic Christian Church*
We believe and profess, one catholic or universal Church, which is a holy congregation, of true Christian believers, all expecting their salvation in Jesus Christ, being washed by his blood, sanctified and sealed by the Holy Ghost. This Church has been from the beginning of the world, and will be to the end thereof; which is evident from this, that Christ is an eternal King, which, without subjects, cannot be. And this holy Church is preserved or supported by God, against the rage of the whole world; though she sometimes (for a while) appears very small, and in the eyes of men, to be reduced to nothing; as during the perilous reign of Ahab, the Lord reserved unto him seven thousand men, who had not bowed their knees to Baal (1 Kings 19:18). Furthermore, this holy Church is not confined, bound, or limited to a certain place or to certain persons, but is spread and dispersed over the whole world; and yet is joined and united with heart and will, by the power of faith, in one and the same spirit.

ARTICLE XXVIII. *That Every One Is Bound to Join Himself to the True Church*

We believe, since this holy congregation is an assembly of those who are saved, and that out of it there is no salvation, that no person of whatsoever state or condition he may be, ought to withdraw himself, to live in a separate state from it; but that all men are in duty bound to join and unite themselves with it; maintaining the unity of the Church; submitting themselves to the doctrine and discipline thereof; bowing their necks under the yoke of Jesus Christ; and as mutual members of the same body, serving to the edification of the brethren, according to the talents God has given them. And that this may be the more effectually observed, it is the duty of all believers, according to the word of God, to separate themselves from all those who do not belong to the Church, and to join themselves to this congregation, wheresoever God has established it, even though the magistrates and edicts of princes were against it, yea, though they should suffer death or any other corporal punishment. Therefore all those, who separate themselves from the same, or do not join themselves to it, act contrary to the ordinance of God.

ARTICLE XXIX. *Of the Marks of the True Church, and Wherein She Differs from the False Church*

We believe, that we ought diligently and circumspectly to discern from the Word of God which is the true Church, since all sects which are in the world assume to themselves the name of the Church. But we speak not here of hypocrites, who are mixed in the Church with the good, yet are not of the Church, though externally in it; but we say that the body and communion of the true Church must be distinguished from all sects, who call themselves the Church. The marks, by which the true Church is known, are these: if the pure doctrine of the gospel is preached therein; if she maintains the pure administration of the sacraments as instituted by Christ; if church discipline is exercised in punishing of sin: in short, if all things are managed according to the pure Word of God, all things contrary thereto corrected, and Jesus Christ acknowledged as the only Head of the Church. Hereby the true Church may certainly be known from which no man has a right to separate himself. With respect to those, who are members of the Church, they may be known by the marks of Christians: namely, by faith; and when they have received Jesus Christ the only Saviour, they avoid sin, follow after righteousness, love the true God and their neighbour, neither turn aside to the right or left, and crucify the flesh with the works thereof. But this is not to be understood, as if there did not remain in them great infirmities; but they fight against them through the Spirit, all the days of their life, continually taking their refuge in the blood, death, passion and obedience of our Lord Jesus Christ, "in whom they have remission of sins, through faith in him." As for the false Church, she ascribes more power and authority to herself and her ordinances than to the Word of God, and will not submit herself to the yoke of Christ. Neither does she administer the sacraments as appointed by Christ in his Word, but adds to and takes from them, as she thinks proper; she relies more upon men than upon Christ; and persecutes those, who live holily according to the Word of God, and rebuke her for her errors, covetousness, and idolatry. These two Churches are easily known and distinguished from each other.

ARTICLE XXX. *Concerning the Government of, and Offices in the Church*

We believe, that this true Church must be governed by that spiritual policy which our Lord has taught us in his Word; namely, that there must be ministers or pastors to preach the Word of God, and to administer the sacraments; also elders and deacons, who, together with the pastors, form the council of the Church: that by these means the true religion may be preserved, and the true doctrine everywhere propagated, likewise transgressors punished and restrained by spiritual means: also that the poor and distressed may be relieved and comforted, according to their necessities. By these means everything will be carried on in the Church with good order and decency, when faithful men are chosen, according to the rule prescribed by St. Paul in his Epistle to Timothy.

ARTICLE XXXI. *Of the Ministers, Elders, and Deacons*

We believe, that the ministers of God's Word, and the elders and deacons, ought to be chosen to their respective offices by a lawful election by the Church, with calling upon the name of the Lord, and in that order which the Word of God teaches. Therefore every one must take heed, not to intrude himself by indecent means, but is bound to wait till it shall please God to call him; that he may have testimony of his calling, and be certain and assured that it is of the Lord. As for the ministers of God's Word, they have equally the same power and authority wheresoever they are, as they are all ministers of Christ, the only universal Bishop, and the only Head of the Church. Moreover, that this holy ordinance of God may not be violated or slighted, we say that every one ought to esteem the ministers of God's Word, and the elders of the Church, very highly for their work's sake, and be at peace with them without murmuring, strife or contention, as much as possible.

ARTICLE XXXII. *Of the Order and Discipline of the Church*

In the meantime we believe, though it is useful and beneficial, that those, who are rulers of the Church, institute and establish certain ordinances among themselves for maintaining the body of the Church; yet they ought studiously to take care, that they do not depart from those things which Christ, our only Master, has instituted. And therefore, we reject all human inventions, and all laws, which man would introduce into the worship of God, thereby to bind and compel the conscience in any manner whatever. Therefore we admit only of that which tends to nourish and preserve concord, and unity, and to keep all men in obedience to God. For this purpose, excommunication or church discipline is requisite, with the several circumstances belonging to it, according to the Word of God.

ARTICLE XXXIII. *Of the Sacraments*

We believe, that our gracious God, on account of our weakness and infirmities has ordained the sacraments for us, thereby to seal unto us his promises, and to be pledges of the good will and grace of God toward us, and also to nourish and strengthen our faith; which he has joined to the Word of the gospel, the better to present to our senses, both that which he signifies to us by his Word, and that which he works inwardly in our hearts, thereby assuring and confirming in us the salvation which he imparts to us. For they are visible signs and seals of an inward and invisible thing, by means whereof God works in us by the power of the Holy Ghost. Therefore the signs are not in vain or insignificant, so as to deceive us. For Jesus Christ is the true object presented by them, without whom they would be of no moment. Moreover, we are satisfied with the number of sacraments which Christ our Lord has instituted, which are two only, namely, the sacrament of baptism, and the holy supper of our Lord Jesus Christ.

ARTICLE XXXIV. *Of Holy Baptism*

We believe and confess that Jesus Christ, who is the end of the law, has made an end, by the shedding of his blood, of all other sheddings of blood which men could or would make as a propitiation or satisfaction for sin and that he, having abolished circumcision, which was done with blood, has instituted the sacrament of baptism instead thereof; by which we are received into the Church of God, and separated from all other people and strange religions, that we may wholly belong to him, whose ensign and banner we bear: and which serves as a testimony to us, that he will forever be our gracious God and Father. Therefore he has commanded all those, who are his, to be baptized with pure water, "in the name of the Father, and of the Son, and of the Holy Ghost": thereby signifying to us, that as water washes away the filth of the body, when poured upon it, and is seen on the body of the baptized, when sprinkled upon him; so does the blood of Christ, by the power of the Holy Ghost, internally sprinkle the soul, cleanse it from its sins, and regenerate us from children of wrath, unto children of God. Not that this is effected by the external water, but by the sprinkling of the precious blood of the Son of God; who is our Red Sea, through which we must pass, to escape the tyranny of Pharaoh, that is, the devil, and to enter into the spiritual land of Canaan. Therefore the ministers, on their part, administer the sacrament, and that which is visible, but our Lord gives that which is signified by the sacrament, namely, the gifts and invisible grace; washing, cleansing and purging our souls of all filth and unrighteousness; renewing our hearts, and filling them with all comfort; giving unto us a true assurance of his fatherly goodness; putting on us the new man, and putting off the old man with all his deeds. Therefore we believe, that every man, who is earnestly studious of obtaining life eternal, ought to be but once baptized with this only baptism, without ever repeating the same: since we cannot be born twice. Neither does this baptism only avail us, at the time when the water is poured upon us, and received by us but also through the whole course of our life; therefore we detest the error of the Anabaptists, who are not content with the one only baptism they have once received, and moreover condemn the baptism of the infants of believers, whom we believe ought to be baptized and sealed with the sign of the covenant, as the children in Israel formerly were circumcised, upon the same promises which are made unto our children. And indeed Christ shed his blood no less for the washing of the children of the faithful, than for adult persons; and therefore they ought to receive the sign and sacrament of that, which Christ has done for them; as the Lord commanded in the law, that they should be made partakers of the sacrament of Christ's suffering and death, shortly after they were born, by offering for them a lamb, which was a sacrament of Jesus Christ. Moreover, what circumcision was to the Jews, that baptism is to our children. And for this reason Paul calls baptism the circumcision of Christ.

ARTICLE XXXV. *Of the Holy Supper of Our Lord Jesus Christ*

We believe and confess, that our Saviour Jesus Christ did ordain and institute the sacrament of the holy supper, to nourish and support those whom he has already regenerated, and incorporated into his family, which is his Church. Now those, who are regenerated, have in them a twofold life, the one corporal and temporal, which they have from the first birth, and is common to all men: the other spiritual and heavenly, which is given them in their second birth, which is effected by the word of the gospel, in the communion of the body of Christ; and this life is not common, but is peculiar to God's elect. In like manner God has given us, for the support of the bodily and earthly life, earthly and common bread, which is subservient thereto, and is common to all men, even to life itself. But for the support of the spiritual and heavenly life, which believers have, he has sent us living bread, which descended from heaven, namely, Jesus Christ, who nourishes and strengthens the spiritual life of believers, when they eat him, that is to say, when they apply and receive him by faith in the spirit. Christ, that he might represent unto us this spiritual and heavenly bread, has instituted an earthly and visible bread, as a sacrament of his body, and wine as a sacrament of his blood, to testify by them unto us, that, as certainly as we receive and hold this sacrament in our hands, and eat and drink the same with our mouths, by which our life is afterwards nourished, we also do as certainly receive by faith (which is the hand and mouth of our soul) the true body and blood of Christ our only Saviour in our souls, for the support of our spiritual life. Now, as it is certain and beyond all doubt, that, that Jesus Christ has not enjoined to us the use of his sacraments in vain, so he works in us all that he represents to us by these holy signs, though the manner surpasses our understanding, and cannot be comprehended by us, as the operations of the Holy Ghost are hidden and incomprehensible. In the meantime we err not, when we say, that what is eaten and drunk by us is the proper and natural body, and the proper blood of Christ. But the manner of our partaking of the same, is not by the mouth, but by the spirit through faith. Thus then, though Christ always sits at the right hand of his Father in the heavens, yet does he not therefore cease to make us partakers of himself by faith. This feast is a spiritual table, at which Christ communicates himself with all his benefits to us, and gives us there to enjoy both himself, and the merits of his sufferings and death, nourishing, strengthening and comforting our poor comfortless souls by the eating of his flesh, quickening and refreshing them by the drinking of his blood. Further, though the sacraments are connected with the thing signified nevertheless both are not received by all men: the ungodly indeed receives the sacrament to his condemnation but he does not receive the truth of the sacrament. As Judas, and Simon the sorcerer, both indeed received the sacrament, but not Christ, who was signified by it, of whom believers only are made partakers. Lastly, we receive this holy sacrament in the assembly of the people of God with humility and reverence, keeping up amongst us the death of Christ our Saviour, with thanksgiving: making there confession of our faith, and of the Christian religion. Therefore no one ought to come to this table without having previously rightly examined himself; lest by eating of this bread and drinking of this cup, he eat and drink judgment to himself. In a word, we are excited by the use of this holy sacrament, to a fervent love towards God and our neighbour. Therefore we reject all mixtures and damnable inventions, which men have added unto, and blended with the sacraments, as profanations of them: and affirm that we ought to rest satisfied with the ordinance which Christ and his apostles have taught us, and that we must speak of them in the same manner as they have spoken.

ARTICLE XXXVI. *Of Magistrates*

We believe that our gracious God, because of the depravity of mankind, has appointed kings, princes and magistrates, willing that the world should be governed by certain laws and policies; to the end that the dissoluteness of men might be restrained and all things carried on among them with good order and decency. For this purpose he has invested the magistracy with the sword, "for the punishment of evildoers, and for the protection of them that do well" (1 Pet. 2:14). And their office is, not only to have regard unto, and watch for the welfare of the civil state; but also that they protect the sacred ministry; and thus may remove and prevent all idolatry and false worship; that the kingdom of antichrist may be thus destroyed and the kingdom of Christ promoted. They must therefore countenance the preaching of the Word of the gospel everywhere, that God may be honoured and worshipped by every one, as he commands in his Word. Moreover, it is the bounden duty of every one, of what state, quality, or condition soever he may be, to subject himself to the magistrates; to pay tribute, to show due honour and respect to them, and to obey them in all things which are not repugnant to the Word of God; to supplicate for them in their prayers, that God may rule and guide them in all their ways, and that we may lead a quiet and peaceable life in all godliness and honesty. Wherefore we detest the Anabaptists and other seditious people, and in general all those who reject the higher powers and magistrates, and would subvert justice, introduce community of goods, and confound that decency and good order, which God has established among men.

ARTICLE XXXVII. *Of the Last Judgment*
Finally we believe, according to the Word of God, when the time appointed by the Lord (which is unknown to all creatures) is come, and the number of the elect complete, that our Lord Jesus Christ will come from heaven, corporally and visibly, as he ascended, with great glory and majesty to declare himself judge of the quick and the dead; burning this old world with fire and flame, to cleanse it. And then all men will personally appear before this great judge, both men and women and children, that have been from the beginning of the world to the end thereof, being summoned by the voice of the archangel, and by the sound of the trumpet of God. For all the dead shall be raised out of the earth, and their souls joined and united with their proper bodies, in which they formerly lived. As for those who shall then be living, they shall not die as the others, but be changed in the twinkling of an eye, and from corruptible, become incorruptible. Then the books (that is to say the consciences) shall be opened, and the dead judged according to what they shall have done in this world, whether it be good or evil. Nay, all men shall give an account of every idle word they have spoken, which the world only counts amusement and jest; and then the secrets and hypocrisy of men shall be disclosed and laid open before all. And therefore the consideration of this judgment, is justly terrible and dreadful to the wicked and ungodly, but most desirable and comfortable to the righteous and elect: because then their full deliverance shall be perfected, and there they shall receive the fruits of their labour and trouble which they have borne. Their innocence shall be known to all, and they shall see the terrible vengeance which God shall execute on the wicked, who most cruelly persecuted, oppressed and tormented them in this world; and who shall be convicted by the testimony of their own consciences, and being immortal, shall be tormented in that everlasting fire, which is prepared for the devil and his angels. But on the contrary, the faithful and elect shall be crowned with glory and honour; and the Son of

God will confess their names before God his Father, and his elect angels; all tears shall be wiped from their eyes; and their cause which is now condemned by many judges and magistrates, as heretical and impious, will then be known to be the cause of the Son of God. And for a gracious reward, the Lord will cause them to possess such a glory, as never entered into the heart of man to conceive. Therefore we expect that great day with a most ardent desire to the end that we may fully enjoy the promises of God in Christ Jesus our Lord. AMEN. "Even so, come, Lord Jesus." —Rev.22:20.

THE HEIDELBERG CATECHISM (1563)
Or Christian Instruction as Conducted in the Churches and Schools of the Electoral Palatinate

Question 1. What is thy only comfort in life and in death?
Answer. That I, with body and soul, both in life and in death, am not my own, but belong to my faithful Savior Jesus Christ, who with His precious blood has fully satisfied for all my sins, and redeemed me from all the power of the devil; and so preserves me, that without the will of my Father in heaven not a hair can fall from my head; yea, that all things must work together for my salvation. Wherefore, by His Holy Spirit, He also assures me of eternal life, and makes me heartily willing and ready henceforth to live unto Him.

Q 2. How many things are necessary for thee to know, that thou in this comfort mayest live and die happily?
A. Three things: first, the greatness of my sin and misery. Second, how I am redeemed from all my sins and misery. Third, how I am to be thankful to God for such redemption.

THE FIRST PART: *Of Man's Misery*

Q 3. Whence knowest thou thy misery?
A. Out of the Law of God.

Q 4. What does the Law of God require of us?
A. Christ teaches us in sum, Matthew 22:37–40, "Thou shalt love the Lord, thy God with all thy heart, and with all thy soul, and with all thy mind, and with all thy strength. This is the first and great commandment; and the second is like unto it: Thou shalt love thy neighbor as thyself. On these two commandments hang all the law and the prophets."

Q 5. Canst thou keep all this perfectly?
A. No: for I am by nature prone to hate God and my neighbor.

Q 6. Did God create man thus wicked and perverse?
A. No, but God created man good, and after His own image, that is, in righteousness and true holiness; that he might rightly know God his Creator, heartily love Him, and live with Him in eternal blessedness, to praise and glorify Him.

Q 7. Whence then comes this depraved nature of man?
A. From the fall and disobedience of our first parents, Adam and Eve, in Paradise, whereby our nature became so corrupt, that we are all conceived and born in sin.

Q 8. But are we so depraved, that we are wholly unapt to any good and prone to all evil?
A. Yes; unless we are born again by the Spirit of God.

Q 9. Does not God then wrong man, by requiring of him in His law that which he cannot perform?

A. No: for God so made man, that he could perform it; but man, through the instigation of the devil, by wilful disobedience deprived himself and all his posterity of this power.

Q 10. Will God suffer such disobedience and apostasy to go unpunished?

A. By no means; but He is terribly displeased with our inborn as well as our actual sins, and will punish them in just judgment in time and eternity, as he has declared: "Cursed is everyone that continueth not in all things which are written in the book of the law, to do them" (Deut. 27:26).

Q 11. Is then God not merciful?

A. God is indeed merciful, but He is likewise just; wherefore His justice requires that sin, which is committed against the most high majesty of God, be also punished with extreme, that is, with everlasting punishment both of body and soul.

THE SECOND PART: *Of Man's Redemption*

Q 12. Since then, by the righteous judgment of God, we deserve temporal and eternal punishment, what is required that we may escape this punishment and be again received into favor?

A. God wills that His justice be satisfied, therefore we must make full satisfaction to the same, either by ourselves or by another.

Q 13. Can we ourselves make this satisfaction?

A. By no means: on the contrary, we daily increase our guilt.

Q 14. Can any mere creature make satisfaction for us?
A. None: for first, God will not punish, in any other creature, that of which man has made himself guilty; and further, no mere creature can sustain the burden of God's eternal wrath against sin, and redeem others therefrom.

Q 15. What manner of mediator and redeemer then must we seek?
A. One who is a true and sinless man, and yet more powerful than all creatures, that is, one who is at the same time true God.

Q 16. Why must He be a true and sinless man?
A. Because the justice of God requires, that the same human nature which has sinned should make satisfaction for sin; but no man, being himself a sinner, could satisfy for others.

Q 17. Why must He be at the same time true God?
A. That by the power of His Godhead He might bear in His manhood the burden of God's wrath and so obtain for and restore to us righteousness and life.

Q 18. But who now is that Mediator, who is at the same time true God and a true, sinless man?
A. Our Lord Jesus Christ, who is freely given unto us for complete redemption and righteousness.

Q 19. Whence knowest thou this?
A. From the Holy Gospel: which God Himself first revealed in Paradise; afterwards proclaimed by the holy Patriarchs and Prophets, and foreshadowed by the sacrifices and other ceremonies of the law; and finally fulfilled by His well-beloved Son.

Q 20. Are all men then saved by Christ, as they have perished in Adam?
A. No; only such as by true faith are ingrafted into Him, and receive all His benefits.

Q 21. What is true faith?
A. It is not only a certain knowledge, whereby I hold for truth all that God has revealed to us in His Word; but also a hearty trust, which the Holy Ghost works in me by the Gospel, that not only to others, but to me also, forgiveness of sins, everlasting righteousness and salvation, are freely given by God, merely of grace, for the sake of Christ's merits.

Q 22. What is then necessary for a Christian to believe?
A. All that is promised us in the Gospel, which the articles of our catholic, undoubted Christian faith teach us in sum.

Q 23. What are these Articles?
A. I believe in God the Father Almighty, Maker of heaven and earth. And in Jesus Christ, His only begotten Son, our Lord: who was conceived by the Holy Ghost, born of the virgin Mary; suffered under Pontius Pilate, was crucified, dead and buried; He descended into hell; the third day He rose from the dead; He ascended into heaven, and sitteth at the right hand of God the Father Almighty; from thence He shall come to judge the quick and the dead.

I believe in the Holy Ghost; the holy catholic Church; the communion of saints; the forgiveness of sins; the resurrection of the body, and the life everlasting.

Q 24. How are these articles divided?
A. Into three parts: the first is of God the Father, and our creation; the second, of God the Son, and our redemption; the third, of God the Holy Ghost, and our sanctification.

Q 25. Since there is but one Divine Being, why speakest thou of three, Father, Son and Holy Ghost?
A. Because God has so revealed Himself in His Word, that these three distinct Persons are the one, true, eternal God.

OF GOD THE FATHER

Q 26. What dost thou believe when thou sayest: I believe in God the Father Almighty, Maker of heaven and earth?
A. That the eternal Father of our Lord Jesus Christ, who of nothing made heaven and earth, with all that in them is, who likewise upholds and governs the same by His eternal counsel and providence, is for the sake of Christ His Son my God and my Father; in whom I so trust, as to have no doubt that He will provide me with all things necessary for body and soul; and further, that whatever evil He sends upon me in this vale of tears He will turn to my good; for He is able to do it, being Almighty God, and willing also, being a faithful Father.

Q 27. What dost thou understand by the Providence of God?
A. The almighty everywhere present power of God, whereby, as it were by His hand, He still upholds heaven and earth, with all creatures; and so governs them, that herbs and grass, rain and drought, fruitful and barren years, meat and drink, health and sickness, riches and poverty, yea, all things, come not by chance, but by His fatherly hand.

Q 28. What does it profit us to know that God has created, and by His providence still upholds all things?
A. That we may be patient in adversity; thankful in prosperity; and for what is future, have good confidence in our faithful God and Father, that no creature shall separate us from His love; since all creatures are so in His hand, that without His will they cannot so much as move.

OF GOD THE SON

Q 29. Why is the Son of God called Jesus, that is, Savior?
A. Because He saves us from our sins; and no salvation is to be either sought or found in any other.

Q 30. Do such then believe in the only Savior Jesus, who seek their salvation and welfare of saints, of themselves, or anywhere else?
A. No; although they may make their boast of Him, yet in act they deny the only Savior Jesus. For either Jesus is not a complete Savior, or they who by true faith receive this Savior, must have in Him all that is necessary to their salvation.

Q 31. Why is He called Christ, that is, Anointed?
A. Because He is ordained of God the Father, and anointed with the Holy Ghost, to be our chief Prophet and Teacher, who fully reveals to us the secret counsel and will of God concerning our redemption; and our only High Priest, who by the one sacrifice of His body has redeemed us, and ever liveth to make intercession for us with the Father; and our eternal King, who governs us by His Word and Spirit, and defends and preserves us in the redemption obtained for us.

Q 32. But why art thou called a Christian?
A. Because by faith I am a member of Christ, and thus a partaker of His anointing; in order that I also may confess His name; may present myself a living sacrifice of thankfulness to Him; and may with free conscience fight against sin and the devil in this life, and hereafter, in eternity, reign with Him over all creatures.

Q 33. Why is He called God's only begotten Son, since we also are the children of God?
A. Because Christ alone is the eternal, natural Son of God; but we are the children of God by adoption through grace for His sake.

Q 34. Why callest thou Him our Lord?
A. Because, not with silver and gold, but with His precious blood, He has redeemed and purchased us, body and soul, from sin and from all the power of the devil, to be His own.

Q 35. What is the meaning of: Conceived by the Holy Ghost, born of the virgin Mary?
A. That the eternal Son of God, who is and continues true and eternal God, took upon Him the very nature of man, of the flesh and blood of the virgin Mary, by the operation of the Holy Ghost; so that He also might be the true seed of David, like unto His brethren in all things, sin excepted.

Q 36. What benefit dost thou receive from the holy conception and birth of Christ?
A. That He is our Mediator, and with His innocence and perfect holiness covers, in the sight of God, my sin, wherein I was conceived.

Q 37. What dost thou understand by the word: Suffered?
A. That all the time He lived on earth, but especially at the end of His life, He bore, in body and soul, the wrath of God against the sin of the whole human race; in order that by His passion, as the only propitiatory sacrifice, He might redeem our body and soul from everlasting damnation, and obtain for us the grace of God, righteousness, and eternal life.

Q 38. Why did He suffer under Pontius Pilate, as judge?

A. That He, being innocent, might be condemned by the temporal judge, and thereby deliver us from the severe judgment of God, to which we are exposed.

Q 39. Is there anything more in His having been crucified, than if He had died some other death?

A. Yes: for thereby I am assured, that He took on Himself the curse which lay upon me; because the death of the cross was accursed of God.

Q 40. Why was it necessary for Christ to suffer death?

A. Because, by reason of the justice and truth of God, satisfaction for our sins could be made no otherwise than by the death of the Son of God.

Q 41. Why was He buried?

A. To show thereby that He was really dead.

Q 42. Since then Christ died for us, why must we also die?

A. Our death is not a satisfaction for our sin, but only a dying to sins and entering into eternal life.

Q 43. What further benefit do we receive from the sacrifice and death of Christ on the cross?

A. That by His power our old man is with Him crucified, slain, and buried; that so the evil lusts of the flesh may no more reign in us, but that we may offer ourselves unto Him a sacrifice of thanksgiving.

Q 44. Why is it added: He descended into Hell?

A. That in my greatest temptations I may be assured that Christ, my Lord, by His inexpressible anguish, pains and terrors, which He suffered in His soul on the cross and before, has redeemed me from the anguish and torment of hell.

Q 45. What benefit do we receive from the Resurrection of Christ?
A. First, by His resurrection He has overcome death, that He might make us partakers of the righteousness which by His death He has obtained for us. Secondly, we also are now by His power raised up to a new life. Thirdly, the resurrection of Christ is to us a sure pledge of our blessed resurrection.

Q 46. How dost thou understand the words: He ascended into Heaven?
A. That Christ, in sight of His disciples, was taken up from the earth into heaven; and in our behalf there continues, until He shall come again to judge the living and the dead.

Q 47. Is not then Christ with us even unto the end of the world, as He has promised?
A. Christ is true Man and true God: according to His human nature, He is now not on earth; but according to His Godhead, majesty, grace, and Spirit, He is at no time absent from us.

Q 48. But are not, in this way, the two natures in Christ separated from one another, if the Manhood be not wherever the Godhead is?
A. By no means; for since the Godhead is incomprehensible and everywhere present, it must follow that it is indeed beyond the bounds of the Manhood, which it has assumed, but is yet nonetheless in the same also, and remains personally united to it.

Q 49. What benefit do we receive from Christ's ascension into Heaven?

A. First, that He is our Advocate in the presence of His Father in heaven. Secondly, that we have our flesh in heaven, as a sure pledge, that He, as the Head, will also take us, His members, up to Himself. Thirdly, that He sends us His Spirit, as an earnest, by whose power we seek those things which are above, where Christ sitteth on the right hand of God, and not things on the earth.

Q 50. Why is it added: And sitteth at the right hand of God?

A. Because Christ ascended into heaven for this end, that He might there appear as Head of His Church, by whom the Father governs all things.

Q 51. What benefit do we receive from this glory of our Head, Christ?

A. First, that by His Holy Spirit He sheds forth heavenly gifts in us, His members; then, that by His power He defends and preserves us against all enemies.

Q 52. What comfort is it to thee, that Christ shall come again to judge the quick and the dead?

A. That in all my sorrows and persecutions, with uplifted head, I look for the selfsame One, who has before offered Himself for me to the judgment of God and removed from me all curse, to come again as Judge from heaven; who shall cast all His and my enemies into everlasting condemnation, but shall take me, with all His chosen ones, to Himself into heavenly joy and glory.

OF GOD THE HOLY GHOST

Q 53. What dost thou believe concerning the Holy Ghost?
A. First, that He is co-eternal God with the Father and the Son. Secondly, that He is also given unto me; makes me by a true faith partaker of Christ and all His benefits; comforts me; and shall abide with me forever.

Q 54. What dost thou believe concerning the Holy Catholic Church?
A. That, out of the whole human race, from the beginning to the end of the world, the Son of God, by His Spirit and Word, gathers, defends, and preserves for Himself unto everlasting life, a chosen communion, in the unity of the true faith; and that I am, and forever shall remain, a living member of the same.

Q 55. What dost thou understand by the Communion of Saints?
A. First, that believers, all and every one, as members of Christ have part in Him and in all His treasures and gifts; secondly, that each one must feel himself bound to use his gifts, readily and cheerfully, for the advantage and welfare of other members.

Q 56. What dost thou believe concerning the Forgiveness of Sins?
A. That God, for the sake of Christ's satisfaction, will no more remember my sins, neither the sinful nature with which I have to struggle all my life long; but graciously imputes to me the righteousness of Christ, that I may nevermore come into condemnation.

Q 57. What comfort does the Resurrection of the Body afford thee?
A. That not only my soul, after this life, shall be immediately taken up to Christ its Head; but also that this my body, raised by the power

of Christ, shall again be united with my soul, and made like unto the glorious body of Christ.

Q 58. What comfort hast thou from the article of the Life Everlasting?

A. That, inasmuch as I now feel in my heart the beginning of eternal joy, I shall after this life possess complete bliss, such as eye hath not seen, nor ear heard, neither hath entered into the heart of man; therein to praise God for ever.

Q 59. But what does it help thee now, that thou believest all this?

A. That I am righteous in Christ before God, and an heir of eternal life.

Q 60. How art thou righteous before God?

A. Only by true faith in Jesus Christ. That is: although my conscience accuse me, that I have grievously sinned against all the commandments of God, and have never kept any of them, and that I am still prone always to all evil, yet God, without any merit of mine, of mere grace, grants and imputes to me the perfect satisfaction, righteousness and holiness of Christ, as if I had never committed nor had any sin, and had myself accomplished all the obedience which Christ has fulfilled for me, if only I accept such benefit with a believing heart.

Q 61. Why sayest thou, that thou art righteous only by faith?

A. Not that I am acceptable to God on account of the worthiness of my faith; but because only the satisfaction, righteousness and holiness of Christ is my righteousness before God, and I can receive the same and make it my own in no other way than by faith only.

Q 62. But why cannot our good works be the whole or part of our righteousness before God?
A. Because the righteousness which can stand before the judgment-seat of God must be perfect throughout and wholly conformable to the divine law; whereas even our best works in this life are all imperfect and defiled with sin.

Q 63. How is it that our good works merit nothing, while yet it is God's will to reward them in this life and in that which is to come?
A. The reward comes not of merit, but of grace.

Q 64. But does not this doctrine make men careless and profane?
A. No, for it is impossible that those who are implanted into Christ by true faith, should not bring forth fruits of thankfulness.

OF THE HOLY SACRAMENTS

Q 65. Since then we are made partakers of Christ and all his benefits by faith only, whence comes this faith?
A. The Holy Ghost works it in our hearts by the preaching of the Gospel, and confirms it by the use of the Holy Sacraments.

Q 66. What are the Sacraments?
A. The Sacraments are visible, holy signs and seals, appointed by God for this end, that by the use thereof He may the more fully declare and seal to us the promise of the Gospel: namely, that He grants us out of free grace the forgiveness of sins and everlasting life, for the sake of the one sacrifice of Christ accomplished on the cross.

Q 67. Are both these, then, the Word and the Sacraments, designed to direct our faith to the sacrifice of Jesus Christ on the cross, as the only ground of our salvation?
A. Yes truly; for the Holy Ghost teaches in the Gospel, and by the Holy Sacraments assures us, that our whole salvation stands in the one sacrifice of Christ made for us on the cross.

Q 68. How many Sacraments has Christ appointed in the New Testament?
A. Two: Holy Baptism and the Holy Supper.

OF HOLY BAPTISM

Q 69. How is it signified and sealed unto thee in Holy Baptism, that thou hast part in the one sacrifice of Christ on the cross?
A. Thus: that Christ has appointed this outward washing with water, and has joined therewith this promise, that I am washed with His blood and Spirit from the pollution of my soul, that is, from all my sins, as certainly, as I am washed outwardly with water, whereby commonly the filthiness of the body is taken away.

Q 70. What is it to be washed with the blood and Spirit of Christ?
A. It is to have the forgiveness of sins from God, through grace, for the sake of Christ's blood, which He shed for us in His sacrifice on the cross; and also, to be renewed by the Holy Ghost, and sanctified to be members of Christ, that so we may more and more die unto sin, and lead holy and unblamable lives.

Q 71. Where has Christ promised that we are as certainly washed with His blood and Spirit as with the water of Baptism?
A. In the institution of Baptism, which runs thus: "Go ye, therefore, and teach all nations, baptizing them in the name of the Father, and

of the Son, and of the Holy Ghost" (Matt. 28:19). "He that believeth and is baptized shall be saved; but he that believeth not shall be damned" (Mk. 16:16). This promise is also repeated where the Scripture calls Baptism the washing of regeneration and the washing away of sins.

Q 72. Is then the outward washing with water itself the washing away of sins?
A. No; for only the blood of Jesus Christ and the Holy Spirit cleanse us from all sin.

Q 73. Why, then, doth the Holy Ghost call Baptism the washing of regeneration, and the washing away of sins?
A. God speaks thus not without great cause: namely, not only to teach us thereby that like as the filthiness of the body is taken away by water, so our sins also are taken away by the blood and Spirit of Christ; but much more, that by this divine pledge and token He may assure us, that we are as really washed from our sins spiritually, as our bodies are washed with water.

Q 74. Are infants also to be baptized?
A. Yes. For since they, as well as their parents, belong to the covenant and people of God, and both redemption from sin and the Holy Ghost, who works faith, are through the blood of Christ promised to them no less than to their parents: they are also by Baptism, as a sign of the covenant, to be ingrafted into the Christian Church, and distinguished from the children of unbelievers, as was done in the Old Testament by Circumcision, in place of which in the New Testament Baptism is appointed.

OF THE HOLY SUPPER OF THE LORD

Q 75. How is it signified and sealed unto thee in the Holy Supper that thou dost partake of the one sacrifice of Christ on the cross and all His benefits?

A. Thus; that Christ has commanded me and all believers to eat of this broken bread, and to drink of this cup, and has joined therewith these promises: First, that His body was offered, and broken on the cross for me, and His blood shed for me, as certainly as I see with my eyes the bread of the Lord broken for me, and the cup communicated to me; and further, that, with His crucified body and shed blood, He Himself feeds and nourishes my soul to everlasting life as certainly as I receive from the hand of the minister, and taste with my mouth, the bread and cup of the Lord, which are given me as certain tokens of the body and blood of Christ.

Q 76. What is it to eat the crucified body and drink the shed blood of Christ?

A. It is not only to embrace with a believing heart all the suffering and death of Christ, and thereby to obtain the forgiveness of sins and eternal life; but moreover also, to be so united more and more to His sacred body by the Holy Ghost, who dwells both in Christ and in us, that although He is in heaven, and we on the earth, we are nevertheless flesh of His flesh and bone of His bones, and live and are governed for ever by one Spirit, as members of the same body are by one soul.

Q 77. Where has Christ promised that He will thus feed and nourish believers with His body and blood, as certainly as they eat of this broken bread and drink of this cup?

A. In the institution of the Supper, which runs thus: "The Lord Jesus Christ, the same night in which he was betrayed, took bread; and when He had given thanks, He brake it, and said: 'Take, eat, this is My body, which is broken for you; this do in remembrance of Me.' After the same manner also He took the cup, when he had supped, saying: 'This cup is the New Testament in My blood: This do ye as often as ye drink it, in remembrance of Me.' For as often as ye eat this bread, and drink this cup, ye do show the Lord's death till He come" (1 Cor. 11:23-26)

And this promise is repeated also by St. Paul, where he says: "The cup of blessing which we bless, is it not the communion of the blood of Christ? The bread which we break, is it not the communion of the body of Christ? For we, being many, are one bread, and one body; for we are all partakers of that one bread" (1 Cor. 10:16).

Q 78. Do then the bread and wine become the real body and blood of Christ?
A. No: but as the water, in Baptism, is not changed into the blood of Christ, nor becomes the washing away of sins itself, being only the divine token and assurance thereof, so also, in the Lord's Supper, the sacred bread does not become the body of Christ itself, though agreeably to the nature and usage of sacraments it is called the body of Christ.

Q 79. Why then doth Christ call the bread His body, and the cup His blood, or the New Testament in His blood; and St. Paul, the communion of the body and blood of Christ?
A. Christ speaks thus not without great cause: namely, not only to teach us thereby, that, like as the bread and wine sustain this temporal life, so also His crucified body and shed blood are the true meat and drink of our souls unto life eternal; but much more, by this visible sign and pledge to assure us, that we are as really partakers of His true body and blood, through the working of the Holy Ghost, as we receive by the mouth of the body these holy tokens in remembrance

of Him; and that all His sufferings and obedience are as certainly our own, as if we had ourselves suffered and done all in our own person.

Q 80. What difference is there between the Lord's Supper and the Popish Mass?
A. The Lord's Supper testifies to us, that we have full forgiveness of all our sins by the one sacrifice of Jesus Christ, which He Himself has once accomplished on the cross; and that by the Holy Ghost we are ingrafted into Christ, who with His true body is now in heaven at the right hand of the Father, and is to be there worshiped. But the Mass teaches, that the living and the dead have not forgiveness of sins through the sufferings of Christ, unless Christ is still daily offered for them by the priests; and that Christ is bodily under the form of bread and wine, and is therefore to be worshiped in them. And thus the Mass at bottom is nothing else than a denial of the one sacrifice and passion of Jesus Christ, and an accursed idolatry.

Q 81. Who are to come unto the table of the Lord?
A. Those who are displeased with themselves for their sins, yet trust that these are forgiven them, and that their remaining infirmity is covered by the passion and death of Christ; who also desire more and more to strengthen their faith and amend their life. But the impenitent and hypocrites eat and drink judgment to themselves.

Q 82. Are they then also to be admitted to this Supper, who show themselves to be, by their confession and life, unbelieving and ungodly?
A. No: for by this the covenant of God is profaned, and His wrath provoked against the whole congregation; wherefore the Christian Church is bound, according to the order of Christ and His Apostles, by the office of the keys to exclude such persons, until they amend their life.

Q 83. What is the Office of the Keys?

A. The Preaching of the Holy Gospel and Church Discipline; by which two things the kingdom of heaven is opened to believers and shut against unbelievers.

Q 84. How is the kingdom of heaven opened and shut by the Preaching of the Holy Gospel?

A. In this way: that according to the command of Christ, it is proclaimed and openly witnessed to believers, one and all, that as often as they accept with true faith the promise of the Gospel, all their sins are really forgiven them of God for the sake of Christ's merits; and on the contrary, to all unbelievers and hypocrites, that the wrath of God and eternal condemnation abide on them, so long as they are not converted; according to which witness of the Gospel, will be the judgment of God both in this life and in that which is to come.

Q 85. How is the kingdom of heaven shut and opened by Church Discipline?

A. In this way: that according to the command of Christ, if any under the Christian name show themselves unsound either in doctrine or life, and after repeated brotherly admonition refuse to turn from their errors of evil ways, they are complained of to the church or to its proper officers, and, if they neglect to hear them also, are by them excluded from the Holy Sacraments and the Christian communion, and by God Himself from the kingdom of Christ; and if they promise and show real amendment, they are again received as members of Christ and His Church.

THE THIRD PART: OF THANKFULNESS

Q 86. Since then we are redeemed from our misery by grace through Christ, without any merit of ours, why must we do good works?

A. Because Christ, having redeemed us by His blood, renews us also by His Holy Spirit after His own image, that with our whole life we may show ourselves thankful to God for His blessing, and that He may be glorified through us; then also, that we ourselves may be assured of our faith by the fruits thereof, and by our godly walk may win others also to Christ.

Q 87. Can they then be saved who do not turn to God from their unthankful, impenitent life?
A. By no means: for, as the Scripture saith, no unchaste person, idolater, adulterer, thief, covetous man, drunkard, slanderer, robber, or any such like, shall inherit the kingdom of God.

Q 88. In how many things does true repentance or conversion consist?
A. In two things: the dying of the old man, and the quickening of the new.

Q 89. What is the dying of the old man?
A. Heartfelt sorrow for sin; causing us to hate and turn from it always more and more.

Q 90. What is the quickening of the new man?
A. Heartfelt joy in God; causing us to take delight in living according to the will of God in all good works.

Q 91. But what are good works?
A. Those only which are done from true faith, according to the Law of God, for His glory; and not such as rest on our own opinion, or the commandments of men.

Q 92. What is the Law of God?
A. God spake all these words, saying:

"I am the Lord thy God, which have brought thee out of the land of Egypt, out of the house of bondage. Thou shalt have no other gods before Me.

"Thou shalt not make unto thee any graven image, or any likeness of anything that is in heaven above or that is in the earth beneath, or that is in the water under the earth; thou shalt not bow down thyself to them, nor serve them. For I the Lord thy God am a jealous God, visiting the iniquity of the fathers upon the children unto the third and fourth generation of them that hate Me; and showing mercy unto thousands of them that love Me, and keep My commandments.

"Thou shalt not take the name of the Lord thy God in vain: for the Lord will not hold him guiltless that taketh His name in vain.

"Remember the Sabbath day to keep it holy. Six days shalt thou labor, and do all thy work: but the seventh day is the Sabbath of the Lord thy God; in it thou shalt not do any work, thou, nor thy son, nor thy daughter, thy manservant, nor thy maidservant, nor thy cattle, nor thy stranger that is within thy gates. For in six days the Lord made heaven and earth, the sea, and all that in them is, and rested the seventh day: wherefore the Lord blessed the Sabbath day, and hallowed it.

"Honor thy father and thy mother; that thy days may be long upon the land which the Lord thy God giveth thee.

"Thou shalt not kill.

"Thou shalt not commit adultery.

"Thou shalt not steal.

"Thou shalt not bear false witness against thy neighbor.

"Thou shalt not covet thy neighbor's house; thou shalt not covet thy neighbor's wife, nor his manservant, nor his maidservant, nor his ox, nor his ass, nor anything that is thy neighbor's."
(Exod. 20:2-17)

Q 93. How are these commandments divided?
A. Into two tables: the first of which teaches us, in four commandments, what duties we owe to God; the second, in six, what duties we owe to our neighbor.

Q 94. What does God require in the first commandment?
A. That, on peril of my soul's salvation, I avoid and flee all idolatry, sorcery, enchantments, invocation of saints or of other creatures; and that I rightly acknowledge the only true God, trust in Him alone, with all humility and patience expect all good from Him only, and love, fear, and honor Him with my whole heart; so as rather to renounce all creatures than do the least thing against His will.

Q 95. What is idolatry?
A. It is instead of the one true God who has revealed Himself in His Word, or along with the same, to conceive or have something else on which to place our trust.

Q 96. What does God require in the second commandment?
A. That we in no wise make any image of God, nor worship Him in any other way than He has commanded in His Word.

Q 97. Must we then not make any image at all?
A. God may not and cannot be imaged in any way; as for creatures, though they may indeed be imaged, yet God forbids the making or keeping any likeness of them, either to worship them, or by them to serve Himself.

Q 98. But may not pictures be tolerated in churches as books for the laity?
A. No: for we should not be wiser than God, who will not have His people taught by dumb idols, but by the lively preaching of His Word.

Q 99. What is required in the third commandment?
A. That we must not by cursing, or by false swearing, nor yet by unnecessary oaths, profane or abuse the name of God; nor even by our silence and connivance be partakers of these horrible sins in others; and in sum, that we use the holy name of God no otherwise than with fear and reverence, so that He may be rightly confessed and worshiped by us, and be glorified in all our words and works.

Q 100. Is then the profaning of God's name by swearing and cursing so grievous a sin that His wrath is kindled against those also who seek not, as much as in them lies, to hinder and forbid the same?
A. Yes truly: for no sin is greater, or more provoking to God than the profaning of His name. Wherefore He even commanded it to be punished with death.

Q 101. But may we not swear by the name of God in a religious manner?
A. Yes; when the magistrate requires it, or it may be needful otherwise to maintain and promote fidelity and truth, to the glory of God and our neighbor's good. For such swearing is grounded in God's Word, and therefore was rightly used by the saints in the Old and New Testaments.

Q 102. May we swear by the saints or any other creature?
A. No: for a lawful oath is a calling upon God, as the only searcher of hearts, to bear witness to the truth, and to punish me if I swear falsely; which honor is due no creature.

Q 103. What does God require in the fourth commandment?
A. In the first place, that the ministry of the Gospel and schools be maintained; and that I, especially on the day of rest, diligently attend church to learn the Word of God, to use the Holy Sacraments, to call

publicly upon the Lord, and to give Christian alms. In the second place, that all the days of my life I rest from my evil works, allow the Lord to work in me by His Spirit, and thus begin in this life the everlasting Sabbath.

Q 104. What does God require in the fifth commandment?
A. That I show all honor, love and faithfulness to my father and mother, and to all in authority over me; submit myself with due obedience to all their good instruction and correction; and also bear patiently with their infirmities: since it is God's will to govern us by their hand.

Q 105. What does God require in the sixth commandment?
A. That I neither in thought, nor in word or look, much less in deed, revile, hate, insult, or kill my neighbor, whether by myself or by another; but lay aside all desire of revenge; moreover, that I harm not myself, nor wilfully run into any danger. Wherefore also, to restrain murder, the magistrate is armed with the sword.

Q 106. But this commandment speaks only of killing?
A. In forbidding this, however, God means to teach us that He abhors the root of murder, namely, envy, hatred, anger, and desire of revenge; and that all these are in His sight hidden murder.

Q 107. Is it then enough that we do not kill our neighbor in any such way?
A. No: for in condemning envy, hatred, and anger, God requires us to love our neighbor as ourselves, to show patience, peace, meekness, mercy, and kindness towards him, and, so far as we have power, to prevent his hurt; also to do good even unto our enemies.

Q 108. What does the seventh commandment teach us?
A. That all unchastity is accursed of God; and that we should therefore loathe it from the heart, and live chastely and modestly whether in holy wedlock or single life.

Q 109. Does God in this commandment forbid nothing more than adultery and such like gross sins?
A. Since our body and soul are both temples of the Holy Ghost, it is His will that we keep both pure and holy; for which reason He forbids all unchaste actions, gestures, words, thoughts, desires, and whatever may entice thereto.

Q 110. What does God forbid in the eighth commandment?
A. Not only such theft and robbery as are punished by the magistrate; but God views as theft all wicked tricks and devices, whereby we seek to draw to ourselves our neighbor's goods, whether by force or with show of right, such as unjust weights, ells, measures, wares, coins, usury, or any means forbidden of God; so moreover all covetousness, and all useless waste of His gifts.

Q 111. But what does God require of thee in this commandment?
A. That I further my neighbor's good, where I can and may; deal with him as I would have others deal with me; and labor faithfully, that I may be able to help the poor in their need.

Q 112. What is required in the ninth commandment?
A. That I bear false witness against no one; wrest no one's words; be no backbiter, or slanderer; join in condemning no one unheard and rashly; but that I avoid, on pain of God's heavy wrath, all lying and deceit, as being the proper works of the devil; in matters of judgment and justice and in all other affairs love, honestly speak and confess the truth; and, so far as I can, defend and promote my neighbor's good name.

Q 113. What is required in the tenth commandment?
A. That not even the least inclination or thought against any of God's commandments ever enter into our heart; but that, with our whole heart, we continually hate all sin, and take pleasure in all righteousness.

Q 114. Can those who are converted to God keep these commandments perfectly?
A. No: but even the holiest men, while in this life, have only a small beginning of this obedience; yet so, that with earnest purpose they begin to live, not only according to some, but according to all the commandments of God.

Q 115. Why then doth God so strictly enjoin upon us the ten commandments, since in this life no one can keep them?
A. First, that all our life long, we may learn more and more to know our sinful nature, and so the more earnestly seek forgiveness of sins and righteousness in Christ; secondly, that we may continually strive, and beg from God the grace of the Holy Ghost, so as to become more and more changed into the image of God, till we attain finally to full perfection after this life.

OF PRAYER

Q 116. Why is Prayer necessary for Christians?
A. Because it is the chief part of the thankfulness which God requires of us; and because God will give His grace and Holy Spirit only to such, as earnestly and without ceasing, beg them from Him, and render thanks unto Him for them.

Q 117. What belongs to such prayer, as God is pleased with and will hear?

A. First, that from the heart we call only upon the one true God, who has revealed Himself to us in His word, for all that He has commanded us to ask of Him; secondly, that we thoroughly know our need and misery, so as to humble ourselves before the face of His Divine Majesty; thirdly, that we be firmly assured, that withstanding our unworthiness He will, for the sake of Christ our Lord, certainly hear our prayer, as He has promised us in His word.

Q 118. What has God commanded us to ask of Him?

A. All things necessary for soul and body, which Christ our Lord has comprised in the prayer taught us by Himself.

Q 119. What is the Lord's Prayer?

A. Our Father which art in heaven: Hallowed by Thy name. Thy kingdom come. Thy will be done in earth, as it is in heaven. Give us this day our daily bread. And forgive us our debts, as we forgive our debtors. And lead us not into temptation; but deliver us from evil. For Thine is the kingdom, and the power, and the glory, for ever. Amen.

Q 120. Why has Christ commanded us to address God thus: Our Father?

A. To awaken in us, at the very beginning of our prayer, that filial reverence and trust toward God, which are to be the ground of our prayer; namely, that God has become our Father through Christ, and will much less deny us what we ask of Him in faith, than our parents refuse us earthly things.

Q 121. Why is it added: Who art in heaven?

A. That we may have no earthly thought of the heavenly majesty of God; and may expect from His almighty power all things necessary for body and soul.

Q 122. What is the first petition?

A. Hallowed be Thy name. That is: Enable us rightly to know Thee, and to hallow, magnify and praise Thee in all Thy works, in which shine forth Thy power, wisdom, goodness, justice, mercy, and truth; and likewise so to order our whole life, in thought, word, and work, that Thy name may not be blasphemed, but honored and praised on our account.

Q 123. What is the second petition?

A. Thy kingdom come. That is: So govern us by Thy word and Spirit, that we submit ourselves unto Thee always more and more; preserve and increase Thy Church; destroy the works of the devil, every power that exalteth itself against Thee, and all wicked devices formed against Thy holy word, until the full coming of Thy kingdom, wherein Thou shalt be all in all.

Q 124. What is the third petition?

A. Thy will be done in earth, as it is in heaven. That is: Grant that we and all men may renounce our own will, and yield ourselves without gainsaying, to Thy will which alone is good; that so every one may fulfill his office and calling, as willingly and truly as the angels do in heaven.

Q 125. What is the fourth petition?

A. Give us this day our daily bread. That is: Be pleased to provide for all our bodily need; that we may thereby know that Thou art the only fountain of all good, and that without Thy blessing, neither our care and labor, nor Thy gifts can profit us; and may therefore withdraw our trust from all creatures, and place it alone in Thee.

Q 126. What is the fifth petition?
A. And forgive us our debts as we forgive our debtors. That is: Be pleased for the sake of Christ's blood, not to impute to us, miserable sinners, our manifold transgressions, nor the evil which still always cleaves to us, as we find this witness of Thy grace in us, that it is our full purpose heartily to forgive our neighbor.

Q 127. What is the sixth petition?
A. And lead us not into temptation; but deliver us from evil. That is: Since we are so weak in ourselves, that we cannot stand a moment; while our deadly enemies, the devil, the world and our own flesh, assail us without ceasing; be pleased to preserve and strengthen us by the power of Thy Holy Spirit, that we may make firm stand against them, and not sink in this spiritual war, until we come off at last with complete victory.

Q 128. How do you close this prayer?
A. For Thine is the kingdom, and the power, and the glory, for ever. That is: All this we ask of Thee, because as our King, having power over all things, Thou art both willing and able to give us all good; and that thereby not we, but Thy holy Name may be glorified for ever.

Q 129. What is the meaning of the word Amen?
A. Amen means: So shall it truly and surely be. For my prayer is much more certainly heard of God, than I feel in my heart that I desire these things of Him.

CANONS OF THE SYNOD OF DORT (1618-19)

FIRST HEAD OF DOCTRINE.
Of Divine Predestination

Article I.
As all men have sinned in Adam, lie under the curse, and are obnoxious to eternal death, God would have done no injustice by leaving them all to perish, and delivering them over to condemnation on account of sin, according to the words of the apostle (Rom. 3:19), "that every mouth may be stopped, and all the world may become guilty before God"; (ver. 23) "for all have sinned, and come short of the glory of God"; and (6:23), "for the wages of sin is death."

Article II.
But "in this the love of God was manifested, that he sent his only-begotten Son into the world," "that whosoever believeth on him should not perish, but have everlasting life" (1 John 4:9; John 3:16).

Article III.
And that men may be brought to believe, God mercifully sends the messengers of these most joyful tidings to whom he will, and at

what time he pleaseth; by whose ministry men are called to repentance and faith in Christ crucified. "How then shall they call on him in whom they have not believed? And how shall they believe in him of whom they have not heard? And how shall they hear without a preacher? And how shall they preach, except they be sent?" (Rom. 10:14, 15).

Article IV.
The wrath of God abideth upon those who believe not this gospel; but such as receive it, and embrace Jesus the Saviour by a true and living faith, are by him delivered from the wrath of God and from destruction, and have the gift of eternal life conferred upon them.

Article V.
The cause or guilt of this unbelief, as well as of all other sins, is nowise in God, but in man himself: whereas faith in Jesus Christ, and salvation through him is the free gift of God, as it is written, "By grace ye are saved through faith, and that not of yourselves: it is the gift of God" (Eph. 3:8); and, "Unto you it is given in the behalf of Christ, not only to believe on him," etc. (Phil. 1:29).

Article VI.
That some receive the gift of faith from God, and others do not receive it, proceeds from God's eternal decree. "For known unto God are all his works from the beginning of the world" (Acts 15:19; Eph. 1:11). According to which decree he graciously softens the hearts of the elect, however obstinate, and inclines them to believe; while he leaves the non-elect in his just judgment to their own wickedness and obduracy. And herein is especially displayed the profound, the merciful, and at the same time the righteous discrimination between men, equally involved in ruin; or that decree of *election* and *reprobation*, revealed in the Word of God, which, though men of perverse, impure,

and unstable minds wrest it to their own destruction, yet to holy and pious souls affords unspeakable consolation.

Article VII.

Election is the unchangeable purpose of God, whereby, before the foundation of the world, he hath, out of mere grace, according to the sovereign good pleasure of his own will, chosen, from the whole human race, which had fallen through their own fault, from their primitive state of rectitude, into sin and destruction, a certain number of persons to redemption in Christ, whom he from eternity appointed the Mediator and head of the elect, and the foundation of salvation.

This elect number, though by nature neither better nor more deserving than others, but with them involved in one common misery, God hath decreed to give to Christ to be saved by him, and effectually to call and draw them to his communion by his Word and Spirit; to bestow upon them true faith, justification, and sanctification; and having powerfully preserved them in the fellowship of his Son, finally to glorify them for the demonstration of his mercy, and for the praise of the riches of his glorious grace: as it is written, "According as he hath chosen us in him before the foundation of the world, that we should be holy and without blame before him in love; having predestinated us unto the adoption of children by Jesus Christ to himself, according to the good pleasure of his will, to the praise of the glory of his grace wherein he hath made us accepted in the Beloved" (Eph. 1:4-6). And elsewhere, "Whom he did predestinate, them he also called; and whom he called, them he also justified; and whom he justified, them he also glorified" (Rom. 8:30).

Article VIII.

There are not various decrees of election, but one and the same decree respecting all those who shall be saved both under the Old and New Testament; since the Scripture declares the good pleasure, purpose, and counsel of the divine will to be one, according to which he hath chosen us from eternity, both to grace and to glory, to salvation and the way of salvation, which he hath ordained that we should walk therein.

Article IX.

This election was not founded upon foreseen faith, and the obedience of faith, holiness, or any other good quality or disposition in man, as the prerequisite, cause, or condition on which it depended; but men are chosen to faith and to the obedience of faith, holiness, etc. Therefore election is the fountain of every saving good; from which proceed faith, holiness, and the other gifts of salvation, and finally eternal life itself, as its fruits and effects, according to that of the apostle. "He hath chosen us [not because we were, but] that we should be holy and without blame before him in love" (Eph. 1:4).

Article X.

The good pleasure of God is the sole cause of this gracious election; which doth not consist herein that God, foreseeing all possible qualities of human actions, elected certain of these as a condition of salvation, but that he was pleased out of the common mass of sinners to adopt some certain persons as a peculiar people to himself, as it is written, "For the children being not yet born, neither having done any good or evil," etc., "it was said [namely, to Rebecca] the elder shall serve the younger; as it is written, Jacob have I loved, but Esau have I hated" (Rom. 9:11-13); and, "As many as were ordained to eternal life believed" (Acts 13:48).

Article XI.

And as God himself is most wise, unchangeable, omniscient, and omnipotent, so the election made by him can neither be interrupted nor changed, recalled nor annulled; neither can the elect be cast away, nor their number diminished.

Article XII.

The elect, in due time, though in various degrees and in different measures, attain the assurance of this their eternal and unchangeable election, not by inquisitively prying into the secret and deep things of God, but by observing in themselves, with a spiritual joy and holy pleasure, the infallible fruits of election pointed out in the Word of God; such as a true faith in Christ, filial fear, a godly sorrow for sin, a hungering and thirsting after righteousness, etc.

Article XIII.

The sense and certainty of this election afford to the children of God additional matter for daily humiliation before him, for adoring the depth of his mercies, and rendering grateful returns of ardent love to him who first manifested so great love towards them. The consideration of this doctrine of election is so far from encouraging remissness in the observance of the divine commands or from sinking men into carnal security, that these, in the just judgment of God, are the usual effects of rash presumption or of idle and wanton trifling with the grace of election, in those who refuse to walk in the ways of the elect.

Article XIV.

As the doctrine of divine election by the most wise counsel of God was declared by the prophets, by Christ himself, and by the apostles, and is clearly revealed in the Scriptures both of the Old and New Testament, so it is still to be published in due time and place in the Church of God, for which it was peculiarly designed, provided it be done with reverence, in the spirit of discretion and piety, for the glory of God's most holy name, and for enlivening and comforting his people, without vainly attempting to investigate the secret ways of the Most High.

Article XV.

What peculiarly tends to illustrate and recommend to us the eternal and unmerited grace of election is the express testimony of sacred

Scripture, that not all, but some only, are elected, while others are passed by in the eternal decree; whom God, out of his sovereign, most just, irreprehensible and unchangeable good pleasure, hath decreed to leave in the common misery into which they have willfully plunged themselves, and not to bestow upon them saving faith and the grace of conversion; but permitting them in his just judgment to follow their own way; at least, for the declaration of his justice, to condemn and punish them forever, not only on account of their unbelief, but also for all their other sins. And this is the decree of reprobation which by no means makes God the author of sin (the very thought of which is blasphemy), but declares him to be an awful, irreprehensible, and righteous judge and avenger.

Article XVI.

Those who do not yet experience a lively faith in Christ, an assured confidence of soul, peace of conscience, an earnest endeavor after filial obedience, and glorying in God through Christ, efficaciously wrought in them, and do nevertheless persist in the use of the means which God hath appointed for working these graces in us, ought not to be alarmed at the mention of reprobation, nor to rank themselves among the reprobate, but diligently to persevere in the use of means, and with ardent desires devoutly and humbly to wait for a season of richer grace. Much less cause have they to be terrified by the doctrine of reprobation, who, though they seriously desire to be turned to God, to please him only, and to be delivered from the body of death, can not yet reach that measure of holiness and faith to which they aspire; since a merciful God has promised that he will not quench the smoking flax, nor break the bruised reed. But this doctrine is justly terrible to those who, regardless of God and of the Saviour Jesus Christ, have wholly given themselves up to the cares of the world and the pleasures of the flesh, so long as they are not seriously converted to God.

Article XVII.

Since we are to judge of the will of God from his Word, which testifies that the children of believers are holy, not by nature, but in virtue of the covenant of grace, in which they together with the parents are comprehended, godly parents have no reason to doubt of the election and salvation of their children whom it pleaseth God to call out of this life in their infancy.

Article XVIII.

To those who murmur at the free grace of election, and just severity of reprobation, we answer with the apostle: "Nay but, O man, who are thou that repliest against God?" (Rom. 9:20); and quote the language of our Saviour: "Is it not lawful for me to do what I will with mine own?" (Matt. 20:15). And therefore with holy adoration of these mysteries, we exclaim, in the words of the apostle: "O the depth of the riches both of the wisdom and knowledge of God! For who hath known the mind of the Lord, or who hath been his counselor? or who hath first given to him, and it shall be recompensed unto him again? For of him, and through him, and to him are all things: to whom be glory forever. Amen" (Rom. 11:33-36).

SECOND HEAD OF DOCTRINE.
Of the Death of Christ, and the Redemption of Men thereby.

Article I.

God is not only supremely merciful, but also supremely just. And his justice requires (as he hath revealed himself in his Word) that our sins committed against his infinite majesty should be punished, not only with temporal, but with eternal punishments, both in body and soul; which we can not escape, unless satisfaction be made to the justice of God.

Article II.

Since, therefore, we are unable to make that satisfaction in our own persons, or to deliver ourselves from the wrath of God, he hath been pleased of his infinite mercy to give his only-begotten Son for our surety, who was made sin, and became a curse for us and in our stead, that he might make satisfaction to divine justice on our behalf.

Article III.

The death of the Son of God is the only and most perfect sacrifice and satisfaction for sin; is of infinite worth and value, abundantly sufficient to expiate the sins of the whole world.

Article IV.

This death derives its infinite value and dignity from these considerations; because the person who submitted to it was not only really man and perfectly holy, but also the only-begotten Son of God, of the same eternal and infinite essence with the Father and Holy Spirit, which qualifications were necessary to constitute him a Saviour for us; and because it was attended with a sense of the wrath and curse of God due to us for sin.

Article V.

Moreover the promise of the gospel is, that whosoever believeth in Christ crucified shall not perish, but have everlasting life. This promise, together with the command to repent and believe, ought to be declared and published to all nations, and to all persons promiscuously and without distinction, to whom God out of his good pleasure sends the gospel.

Article VI.

And, whereas many who are called by the gospel do not repent nor believe in Christ, but perish in unbelief; this is not owing to any defect or insufficiency in the sacrifice offered by Christ upon the cross, but is wholly to be imputed to themselves.

Article VII.
But as many as truly believe, and are delivered and saved from sin and destruction through the death of Christ, are indebted for this benefit solely to the grace of God given them in Christ from everlasting, and not to any merit of their own.

Article VIII.
For this was the sovereign counsel and most gracious will and purpose of God the Father, that the quickening and saving efficacy of the most precious death of his Son should extend to all the elect, for bestowing upon them alone the gift of justifying faith, thereby to bring them infallibly to salvation: that is, it was the will of God, that Christ by the blood of the cross, whereby he confirmed the new covenant, should effectually redeem out of every people, tribe, nation, and language, all those, and those only, who were from eternity chosen to salvation, and given to him by the Father; that he should confer upon them faith, which, together with all the other saving gifts of the Holy Spirit, he purchased for them by his death; should purge them after believing; and having faithfully preserved them even to the end, should at last bring them free from every spot and blemish to the enjoyment of glory in his own presence forever.

Article IX.
This purpose proceeding from everlasting love towards the elect, has, from the beginning of the world to this day, been powerfully accomplished, and will, henceforward, still continue to be accomplished, notwithstanding all the ineffectual opposition of the gates of hell; so that the elect in due time may be gathered together

into one, and that there never may be wanting a Church composed of believers, the foundation of which is laid in the blood of Christ, which may steadfastly love and faithfully serve him as their Saviour, who, as a bridegroom for his bride, laid down his life for them upon the cross; and which may celebrate his praises here and through all eternity.

THIRD AND FOURTH HEADS OF DOCTRINE.
Of the Corruption of Man, his Conversion to God, and the Manner thereof.

Article I.
Man was originally formed after the image of God. His understanding was adorned with a true and saving knowledge of his Creator, and of spiritual things; his heart and will were upright, all his affections pure, and the whole Man was holy; but revolting from God by the instigation of the devil, and abusing the freedom of his own will, he forfeited these excellent gifts, and on the contrary entailed on himself blindness of mind, horrible darkness, vanity, and perverseness of judgment; became wicked, rebellious, and obdurate in heart and will, and impure in [all] his affections.

Article II.
Man after the fall begat children in his own likeness. A corrupt stock produced a corrupt offspring. Hence all the posterity of Adam, Christ only excepted, have derived corruption from their original parent, not by imitation, as the Pelagians of old asserted, but by the propagation of a vicious nature.

Article III.

Therefore all men are conceived in sin, and are by nature children of wrath, incapable of any saving good, prone to evil, dead in sin, and in bondage thereto; and, without the regenerating grace of the Holy Spirit, they are neither able nor willing to return to God, to reform the depravity of their nature, nor to dispose themselves to reformation.

Article IV.

There remain, however, in man since the fall, the glimmerings of natural light, whereby he retains some knowledge of God, of natural things, and of the difference between good and evil, and discovers some regard for virtue, good order in society, and for maintaining an orderly external deportment. But so far is this light of nature from being sufficient to bring him to a saving knowledge of God, and to true conversion, that he is incapable of using it aright even in things natural and civil. Nay farther, this light, such as it is, man in various ways renders wholly polluted, and holds it in unrighteousness; by doing which he becomes inexcusable before God.

Article V.

In the same light are we to consider the law of the decalogue, delivered by God to his peculiar people the Jews, by the hands of Moses. For though it discovers the greatness of sin, and more and more convinces man thereof, yet as it neither points out a remedy nor imparts strength to extricate him from misery, and thus being weak through the flesh, leaves the transgressor under the curse, man can not by this law obtain saving grace.

Article VI.

What, therefore, neither the light of nature nor the law could do, that God performs by the operation of his Holy Spirit through the word or ministry of reconciliation: which is the glad tidings concerning the Messiah, by means whereof it hath pleased God to save such as believe, as well under the Old as under the New Testament.

Article VII.

This mystery of his will God discovered to but a small number under the Old Testament; under the New, he reveals himself to many, without any distinction of people. The cause of this dispensation is not to be ascribed to the superior worth of one nation above another, nor to their making a better use of the light of nature, but results wholly from the sovereign good pleasure and unmerited love of God. Hence they to whom so great and so gracious a blessing is communicated, above their desert, or rather notwithstanding their demerits, are bound to acknowledge it with humble and grateful hearts, and with the apostle to adore, not curiously to pry into the severity and justice of God's judgments displayed in others, to whom this grace is not given.

Article VIII.

As many as are called by the gospel are unfeignedly called; for God hath most earnestly and truly declared in his Word what will be acceptable to him, namely, that all who are called should comply with the invitation. He, moreover, seriously promises eternal life and rest to as many as shall come to him, and believe on him.

Article IX.

It is not the fault of the gospel, nor of Christ offered therein, nor of God, who calls men by the gospel, and confers upon them various gifts, that those who are called by the ministry of the Word refuse to come and be converted. The fault lies in themselves; some of whom when called, regardless of their danger, reject the Word of life; others, though they receive it, suffer it not to make a lasting impression on their heart; therefore, their joy, arising only from a temporary faith, soon vanishes, and they fall away; while others choke the seed of the Word by perplexing cares and the pleasures of this world, and produce no fruit. This our Saviour teaches in the parable of the sower (Matt. 13).

Article X.

But that others who are called by the gospel obey the call and are converted, is not to be ascribed to the proper exercise of free will, whereby one distinguishes himself above others equally furnished with grace sufficient for faith and conversion (as the proud heresy of Pelagius maintains); but it must be wholly ascribed to God, who, as he hath chosen his own from eternity in Christ, so he confers upon them faith and repentance, rescues them from the power of darkness, and translates them into the kingdom of his own Son, that they may show forth the praises of him who hath called them out of darkness into his marvelous light; and may glory not in themselves but in the Lord, according to the testimony of the apostles in various places.

Article XI.

But when God accomplishes his good pleasure in the elect, or works in them true conversion, he not only causes the gospel to be externally preached to them, and powerfully illuminates their minds by his Holy Spirit, that they may rightly understand and discern the things of the Spirit of God, but by the efficacy of the same regenerating Spirit he pervades the inmost recesses of the man; he opens the closed and softens the hardened heart, and circumcises that which was uncircumcised; infuses new qualities into the will, which, though heretofore dead, he quickens; from being evil, disobedient, and refractory, he renders it good, obedient, and pliable; actuates and strengthens it, that, like a good tree, it may bring forth the fruits of good actions.

Article XII.

And this is the regeneration so highly celebrated in Scripture and denominated a new creation: a resurrection from the dead; a making alive, which God works in us without our aid. But this is nowise effected merely by the external preaching of the gospel, by moral suasion, or such a mode of operation that, after God has performed his part, it still remains in the power of man to be regenerated or not, to be converted or to continue unconverted; but it is evidently a supernatural work, most powerful, and at the same time most delightful, astonishing, mysterious, and ineffable; not inferior in efficacy to creation or the resurrection from the dead, as the Scriptures inspired by the author of this work declares; so that all in whose hearts God works in this marvelous manner are certainly, infallibly, and effectually regenerated, and do actually believe. Whereupon the will thus renewed is not only actuated and influenced by God, but, in consequence of this influence, becomes itself active. Wherefore, also, man is himself rightly said to believe and repent, by virtue of that grace received.

Article XIII.

The manner of this operation can not be fully comprehended by believers in this life. Notwithstanding which, they rest satisfied with knowing and experiencing that by this grace of God they are enabled to believe with the heart and to love their Saviour.

Article XIV.

Faith is therefore to be considered as the gift of God, not on account of its being offered by God to man, to be accepted or rejected at his pleasure, but because it is in reality conferred, breathed, and infused into him; nor even because God bestows the power or ability to believe, and then expects that man should, by the exercise of his own free will, consent to the terms of salvation, and actually believe in Christ; but because he who works in man both to will and to do, and indeed all things in all, produces both the will to believe and the act of believing also.

Article XV.

God is under no obligation to confer this grace upon any; for how can he be indebted to man, who had no previous gift to bestow as a foundation for such recompense? Nay, who has nothing of his own but sin and falsehood. He, therefore, who becomes the subject of this grace owes eternal gratitude to God, and gives him thanks forever. Whoever is not made partaker thereof is either altogether regardless of these spiritual gifts and satisfied with his own condition, or is in no apprehension of danger, and vainly boasts the possession of that which he has not. With respect to those who make an external profession of faith and live regular lives, we are bound, after the example of the apostle, to judge and speak of them in the most favorable manner; for the secret recesses of the heart are unknown to us. And as to others, who have not yet been called, it is our duty as though they were. But we are in no wise to conduct ourselves toward them with haughtiness, as if we had made ourselves to differ.

Article XVI.

But as man by the fall did not cease to be a creature endowed with understanding and will, nor did sin, which pervaded the whole race of mankind, deprive him of the human nature, but brought upon him depravity and spiritual death; so also this grace of regeneration does not treat men as senseless stocks and blocks, nor take away their will and its properties, neither does violence thereto; but spiritually quickens, heals, corrects, and at the same time sweetly and powerfully bends it, that where carnal rebellion and resistance formerly prevailed a ready and sincere spiritual obedience begins to reign; in which the true and spiritual restoration and freedom of our will consist. Wherefore, unless the admirable Author of every good work wrought in us, man could have no hope of recovering from his fall by his own free will, by the abuse of which, in a state of innocence, he plunged himself into ruin.

Article XVII.
As the almighty operation of God, whereby he prolongs and supports this our natural life, does not exclude, but requires the use of means, by which God of his infinite mercy and goodness hath chosen to exert his influence; so also the before-mentioned supernatural operation of God, by which we are regenerated, in nowise excludes or subverts the use of the gospel, which the most wise God has ordained to be the seed of regeneration and food of the soul. Wherefore as the apostles, and the teachers who succeeded them, piously instructed the people concerning this grace of God, to his glory and the abasement of all pride, and in the mean time, however, neglected not to keep them by the sacred precepts of the gospel, in the exercise of the Word, the sacraments and discipline; so, even to this day, be it far from either instructors or instructed to presume to tempt God in the Church by separating what he of his good pleasure hath most intimately joined together. For grace is conferred by means of admonitions; and the more readily we perform our duty, the more eminent usually is this blessing of God working in us, and the more directly is his work advanced; to whom alone all the glory, both of means and their saving fruit and efficacy, is forever due. Amen.

FIFTH HEAD OF DOCTRINE.
Of the Perseverance of the Saints.

Article I.
Whom God calls, according to his purpose, to the communion of his Son our Lord Jesus Christ, and regenerates by the Holy Spirit, he delivers also from the dominion and slavery of sin in this life; though

not altogether from the body of sin and from the infirmities of the flesh, so long as they continue in this world.

Article II.

Hence spring daily sins of infirmity, and hence spots adhere to the best works of the saints, which furnish them with constant matter for humiliation before God, and flying for refuge to Christ crucified; for mortifying the flesh more and more by the spirit of prayer and by holy exercises of piety; and for pressing forward to the goal of perfection, till being at length delivered from this body of death, they are brought to reign with the Lamb of God in heaven.

Article III.

By reason of these remains of indwelling sin, and the temptations of sin and of the world, those who are converted could not persevere in a state of grace if left to their own strength. But God is faithful, who having conferred grace, mercifully confirms and powerfully preserves them therein, even to the end.

Article IV.

Although the weakness of the flesh can not prevail against the power of God, who confirms and preserves true believers in a state of grace, yet converts are not always so influenced and actuated by the Spirit of God as not in some particular instances sinfully to deviate from the guidance of divine grace, so as to be seduced by, and to comply with, the lusts of the flesh; they must therefore be constant in watching and prayer, that they be not led into temptation. When these are neglected, they are not only liable to be drawn into great and heinous sins by Satan, the world, and the flesh, but sometimes by the righteous permission of God actually fall into these evils. This the lamentable fall of David, Peter, and other saints described in Holy Scriptures, demonstrates.

Article V.

By such enormous sins, however, they very highly offend God, incur a deadly guilt, grieve the Holy Spirit, interrupt the exercise of faith, very grievously wound their consciences, and sometimes lose the sense of God's favor, for a time, until on their returning into the right way by serious repentance, the light of God's fatherly countenance again shines upon them.

Article VI.

But God, who is rich in mercy, according to his unchangeable purpose of election does not wholly withdraw the Holy Spirit from his own people, even in their melancholy falls; nor suffer them to proceed so far as to lose the grace of adoption and forfeit the state of justification, or to commit the sin unto death; nor does he permit them to be totally deserted, and to plunge themselves into everlasting destruction.

Article VII.

For in the first place, in these falls he preserves in them the incorruptible seed of regeneration from perishing or being totally lost; and again, by his Word and Spirit, he certainly and effectually renews them to repentance, to a sincere and godly sorrow for their sins, that they may seek and obtain remission in the blood of the Mediator, may again experience the favor of a reconciled God, through faith adore his mercies, and henceforward more diligently work out their own salvation with fear and trembling.

Article VIII.

Thus, it is not in consequence of their own merits or strength, but of God's free agency, that they do not totally fall from faith and grace, nor continue and perish finally in their backslidings; which, with respect to themselves is not only possible, but would undoubtedly happen; but with respect to God, it is utterly impossible, since his counsel cannot be changed, nor his promise fail, neither can the call according to his purposed be revoked, nor the merit, intercession, and preservation of Christ be rendered ineffectual, nor the sealing of the Holy Spirit be frustrated or obliterated.

Article IX.

Of this preservation of the elect to salvation, and of their perseverance in the faith, true believers for themselves may and do arrive at the certain persuasion that they ever will continue true and living members of the Church; and that they experience forgiveness of sins, and will at last inherit eternal life.

Article X.

This assurance, however, is not produced by any peculiar revelation contrary to, or independent of the Word of God, but springs from faith in God's promises, which he has most abundantly revealed in his Word for our comfort; from the testimony of the Holy Spirit, witnessing with our spirits, that we are children and heirs of God (Rom. 8:16); and, lastly, from a serious and holy desire to preserve a good conscience, and to perform good works. And if the elect of God were deprived of this solid comfort, that they shall finally obtain the victory, and of this infallible pledge or earnest of eternal glory, they would be of all men the most miserable.

Article XI.

The Scripture moreover testifies that believers in this life have to struggle with various carnal doubts, and that under grievous temptations they are not always sensible of this full assurance of faith and certainty of persevering. But God, who is the Father of all consolation, does not suffer them to be tempted above that they are able, but will with the temptation also make a way to escape, that they may be able to bear it (1 Cor. 10:13); and by the Holy Spirit again inspires them with the comfortable assurance of persevering.

Article XII.

This certainty of perseverance, however, is so far from exciting in believers a spirit of pride, or of rendering them carnally secure, that, on the contrary, it is the real source of humility, filial reverence, true piety, patience in every tribulation, fervent prayers, constancy in suffering and in confessing the truth, and of solid rejoicing in God; so that the consideration of this benefit should serve as an incentive to the serious and constant practice of gratitude and good works, as appears from the testimonies of Scripture and the examples of the saints.

Article XIII.

Neither does renewed confidence of persevering produce licentiousness or a disregard to piety in those who are recovered from backsliding; but it renders them much more careful and solicitous to continue in the ways of the Lord, which he hath ordained, that they who walk therein may maintain an assurance of persevering; lest by abusing his fatherly kindness, God should turn away his gracious countenance from them (to behold which is to the godly dearer than life, the withdrawing whereof is more bitter than death), and they in consequence thereof should fall into more grievous torments of conscience.

Article XIV.

And as it hath pleased God, by the preaching of the gospel, to begin this work of grace in us, so he preserves, continues, and perfects it by the hearing and reading of his Word, by meditation thereon, and by the exhortations, threatenings, and promises thereof, as well as by the used of the Sacraments.

Article XV.

The carnal mind is unable to comprehend this doctrine of the perseverance of the saints, and the certainty thereof, which God hath most abundantly revealed in his Word, for the glory of his name and the consolation of pious souls, and which he impresses upon the hearts of the faithful. Satan abhors it; the world ridicules it; the ignorant and hypocrite abuse, and heretics oppose it. But the spouse of Christ hath always most tenderly loved and constantly defended it, as an inestimable treasure; and God, against whom neither counsel nor strength can prevail, will dispose her to continue this conduct to the end. Now to this one God, Father, Son, and Holy Spirit be honor and glory forever. Amen.

CONCLUSION

And this is the perspicuous, simple, and ingenuous declaration of the orthodox doctrine respecting the five articles which have been controverted in the Belgic churches; and the rejection of the errors, with which they have for some time been troubled. This doctrine the Synod judges to be drawn from the Word of God, and to be agreeable to the confessions of the Reformed churches. Whence it clearly appears that some, whom such conduct by no means became, have violated all truth, equity, and charity, in wishing to persuade the public:

"That the doctrine of the Reformed churches concerning predestination, and the points annexed to it, by its own genius and necessary tendency, leads off the minds of men from all piety and religion; that it is an opiate administered by the flesh and the devil; and the stronghold of Satan, where he lies in wait for all, and from which he wounds multitudes, and mortally strikes through many with the darts both of despair and security; that it makes God the author of sin, unjust, tyrannical, hypocritical; that it is nothing more than interpolated Stoicism, Manicheism, Libertinism, Turcism; that it renders men carnally secure, since they are persuaded by it that nothing can hinder the salvation of the elect, let them live as they please; and, therefore, that they may safely perpetrate every species of the most atrocious crimes; and that, if the reprobate should even perform truly all the works of the saints, their obedience would not in the least contribute to their salvation; that the same doctrine teaches that God, by a mere arbitrary act of his will, without the least respect or view to any sin, has predestinated the greatest part of the world to eternal damnation, and has created them for this very purpose; that in the same manner in which the election is the fountain and cause of faith and good works, reprobation is the cause of unbelief and impiety; that many children of the faithful are torn guiltless from their mothers' breasts and tyrannically plunged into hell: so that neither baptism nor the prayers of the Church at their baptism can at all profit them"; and many other things of the same kind which the Reformed churches not only do not acknowledge, but even detest with their whole soul.

Wherefore, this Synod of Dort, in the name of the Lord, conjures as many as piously call upon the name of our Saviour Jesus Christ to judge the faith of the Reformed churches, not from the calumnies which on every side are heaped upon it, nor from the private expressions of a few among ancient and modern teachers, often dishonestly quoted, or corrupted and wrested to a meaning quite foreign to their intention; but from the public confessions of the churches themselves, and from this declaration of the orthodox doctrine, confirmed by the unanimous consent of all and each of the members of the whole Synod. Moreover, the Synod warns calumniators themselves to consider the terrible judgment of God which awaits them, for bearing false witness against the confessions of so many churches; for distressing the consciences of the weak; and for laboring to render suspected the society of the truly faithful.

Finally, this Synod exhorts all their brethren in the gospel of Christ to conduct themselves piously and religiously in handling this doctrine, both in the universities and churches; to direct it, as well in discourse as in writing to the glory of the Divine name, to holiness of life, and to the consolation of afflicted souls; to regulate, by the Scripture, according to the analogy of faith, not only their sentiments, but also their language, and to abstain from all those phrases which exceed the limits necessary to be observed in ascertaining the genuine sense of the Holy Scriptures, and may furnish insolent sophists with a just pretext for violently assailing or even vilifying, the doctrine of the Reformed churches.

May Jesus Christ, the Son of God, who, seated at the Father's right hand, gives gifts to men, sanctify us in the truth; bring to the truth those who err; shut the mouths of the calumniators of sound doctrine, and endue the faithful ministers of his Word with the spirit of wisdom and discretion, that all their discourses may tend to the glory of God, and the edification of those who hear them. Amen.

Made in the USA
Monee, IL
16 April 2026